New Testament Themes

David A. deSilva

ST. LOUIS, MISSOURI

Cover art and design: Grady Gunter
Interior design: Wynn Younker
Art direction: Elizabeth Wright

Visit Chalice Press on the World Wide Web at
www.chalicepress.com

10 9 8 7 6 5 4 3 2 06 07 08 09 10 11

Library of Congress Cataloging–in–Publication Data

DeSilva, David Arthur.
New Testament Themes / David A. deSilva.
p. cm.
Includes bibliographical references and indexes.
ISBN-13: 978-0-827225-11-4
ISBN-10: 0-827225-11-3
1. Bible. N.T.–Theology I. Title.
BS2397 .D47 2001
225.6 – dc21 00-011579

Printed in the United States of America

For my parents,
Dr. J. Arthur deSilva and Mrs. Dorothy A. deSilva,
in honor of their fortieth wedding anniversary

Contents

Introduction

Although the Christian church has looked to a varied collection of texts as its sacred scripture, Christians have nevertheless sensed a fundamental core message within those texts. Written across a span of five or more decades and addressing widely differing situations and audiences, the texts that came to make up the New Testament were brought together out of a conviction that they contained a basic coherence that could provide guidance to the growing church with regard to its identity, its relationships, and its future.

The goal of this book is to explore those themes that give coherence and consistency to the New Testament. Rather than focus on introducing each text in its historical setting or developing a history of early Christian thought, this book will pursue the way in which a particular theme is developed throughout the New Testament. The reader should hope to leave this book with a clear sense of that thought-world and ethos in which the early Christian would have been immersed as he or she came to join the Christian movement and was nurtured by the voices that the New Testament would come to comprise.

The first theme is "The Favor of God." The Christian movement as a whole began as a response to what was perceived as a new outpouring of God's favor on humanity. The New Testament authors are careful to connect this manifestation of God's favor with God's promises to God's historic people, Israel, but also to underscore the ways in which they are witnessing a more decisive and broader manifestation of God's generosity than any known previously. Of particular importance is the role of Jesus of Nazareth as the mediator through whom God's favor is secured and God's gifts enjoyed. The many facets of God's gift are also developed in different ways.

While much of the New Testament speaks of God's favor, an equally important theme is "The Way of God," that life of discipleship into which the recipient of favor is called. In the ancient world, an act of gift giving is not completed when it is received, but when it is returned. The early Christian teachers thought no differently from their world on this point, and so they highlight the importance of responding to God's favor in a manner that shows reverence for the gift and gratitude toward the Giver.

Modern Western Christianity may suffer from individualism, but the New Testament authors understood that God's favor meant the formation of a community, "The People of God." The early Christians were deeply interested in the way in which this new community was related to Israel, the historic people of God, particularly since by the end of the first century it was clear that synagogue and church would have to live side by side, neither swallowing up the other. The experience of community was itself central to the early church, both in its gathering for worship and in its attempt to live out the ideal of "sibling love" within this new family of the "many sons and daughters" formed by God and joined to the Son.

Finally, the Christian community looked ahead to "The Triumph of God." The backdrop of everyday life was the cosmic struggle between God and the minions of evil, playing itself out in the human scene in the struggle of Christians to resist sin and the unbelieving society. A decisive moment in this contest was the death and resurrection of Jesus, which sounded the beginning of the end. The New Testament authors therefore position their congregations between the beginning of God's final triumph and its final consummation. The early Christians were thus led to view their daily lives against the backdrop of a cosmic contest, in which they were invited to participate by resisting all the forces that opposed God, and against the backdrop of God's coming in judgment and final triumph, when they would also receive the greatest gifts that God had promised them.

Although we shall explore these themes one at a time, they are far from being separate from one another. Rather than thinking of them as four distinct bodies of New Testament teaching, the reader should regard them as four aspects of entry into a coherent worldview and value system that came to characterize early Christianity. They provide a natural, flowing sequence: the announcement of God's favor, the individual's response of gratitude to this display of favor, the mutual obligations within and the character of the community of those who stand in God's favor, and the future of the community of those disciples called "in grace."Certainly, the decision to limit the discussion to four themes is somewhat arbitrary. Furthermore, another reader of the New Testament might choose to name the themes or divide the subject matter quite differently. Nevertheless, through these particular four portals we can see the greater part of the vistas envisioned in the New Testament. It will lie with the reader to decide if the discussion has adequately drawn out the coherence of the texts in a way that explains why the early church chose and treasured these twenty-seven texts above all others as the means by which they could shape their identity, ethos, and hope.

This book is directed primarily to the beginning student of the New Testament, whether that person is enrolled in school or is a layperson in the church. I have therefore dispensed with the scholarly apparatus of footnotes, but in the bibliography at the end of the book I direct the reader to the works that I have found most helpful in my own research. The bibliography may be taken as suggestions for further reading on the historical setting and social world of the New Testament (which for reasons of space and scope could not be discussed here), as well as on the four themes themselves. Many key texts are discussed in the body of this book, but many more are cited merely as references. The reader is strongly encouraged to look up and read these references as she or he progresses through the book as a means of deepening the experience of seeing how the threads of the New Testament create the tapestry of each theme. It will make reading the book a longer exercise but, in the end, a far more rewarding one.

CHAPTER 1

Grace

The Favor of God

If one were to choose a single word to characterize the message of the New Testament, one might be led to select the word *grace.* A large percentage of these writings are dedicated to speaking about a new pouring out of God's favor, a divine initiative to which the early church and its writings are but a response. The authors of the New Testament characterize the present as the time of God's favor, of God's remembrance of God's promises to benefit God's people, and of the enacting of the fulfillment of those promises. The book of Acts presents the history of the early church as an unfolding of God's grace at every turn. Almost every New Testament letter opens and closes with the prayer that God's favor (grace) be on the hearers. The commitment of Paul and Paul's team to keeping God's grace in the center of the gospel message is also well known. They speak of the Christians as those who stand "in grace (Rom. 5:1–2; Gal. 1:6) and of God's grace, or favor, as the foundation of the Christian hope and life (Gal. 2:20–21; Eph. 2:4–10).

An emphasis on grace is certainly not unique to Christianity: The Israelites also understood their covenant with God to have been initiated by God's desire to benefit them and not caused by any claim they had on God. The attempt to characterize the

Old Testament as "Law" and the New Testament as "Grace" is but a caricature of Israelite religion. The fact that the early Christians could view their own experience of God's favor as a "New Covenant" displays an understanding of "Covenant" itself as an act of favor. It was vitally important for the authors of the New Testament to lay out the essential continuity between God's favor toward the historic people of God (Israel) and the new outpouring of God's favor "in these last days" (Heb. 1:2). What is distinctive about God's favor in the New Testament is the way in which it has been offered and secured, namely through the person Jesus, and the scope of God's favor, now reaching out to Jew and Gentile on an equal basis rather than in a way that preserves ethnic boundaries.

All four themes included in this book, moreover, depend in large measure on this first theme, the favor of God. It is in response to the experience of God's favor that a person pursues a life of discipleship, in which he or she seeks to honor, serve, and remain loyal to this divine Benefactor. An important facet of God's favor is adoption into God's people, even into God's own family, bringing one into relation with a body of people toward whom one has the obligations of close kin (and from whom one can hope for the love and support characteristic of close-knit families). Finally, God's favor encompasses not only present gifts but even greater promises for the future, calling the community of disciples to live life looking ahead to God's triumph and the consummation of God's generosity toward the loyal in the age to come. Seen from these various angles, then, grace certainly commends itself as a foundational and primary theme giving coherence to the New Testament message.

The Context of "Grace"

The New Testament authors, wishing to speak of their experience of God, chose a word that already had a well-developed and well-defined social context. "Grace" (*charis*) was not a word invented by Christians (or by anyone in a religious context): It had long been used to speak of the ways in which generous people interacted with their city and with those of lesser means, as well as the way in which committed friends interacted with one another. It was the language of the exchange of favors, of the giving of assistance and the returning of gratitude.

In the classical world, including the world of the first century, a person frequently had to rely on the goodwill and generosity of another in order to get what he or she needed or desired. For example, a poor harvest might imperil a peasant family, so the head of the house would seek assistance from a person of greater means so that his family would have food and seed to try again the next year. A young member of the elite, harboring ambitions of participating in government, might seek the tutelage and assistance of a senior and experienced statesman. A person in danger from others might seek protection from a more powerful person. *Grace* in this context referred first to the favorable disposition of the benefactor: If he or she were disposed to meet the needs of the one who sought help, this would be *grace.* The same word could also be used for the gifts themselves. Finally, and rather surprisingly, *grace* was also used to name the response of the one who received help. We would use the word *gratitude* to capture this aspect of grace.

Grace language was employed in three basic kinds of relationships. First was the rather impersonal generosity displayed when a rich citizen provided entertainment (for example, paying for local athletic contests) or public improvements (sidewalks, public buildings, and the like) for the city. Such benefactors would receive the respect of their fellow citizens and often some public commemoration, such as an inscription, but no personal bonds were formed between the benefactor and the citizenry at large. Second was a more personal kind of patronage, in which a person of means met the need of an individual or family. Here, the patron's grace would initiate a potentially long-term relationship between himself or herself and the clients whom he or she helped. The beneficiaries would become part of the extended household of the patron, to whom they would have recourse in the future as needs arose; they would also remain obliged to honor their patron, to remain loyal to this person, and to offer what services they could. Finally, there was the exchange of favors between social equals, who would call themselves "friends" of one another. These would also display loyalty to one another, but the nature of their assistance was the mutual aid of peers.

These grace relationships were also regulated by a well-defined code of conduct. The fact that moralists frequently wrote about this code and sought to guard against breaches of it tells us that it was not always followed, but there was at least an "ideal" in the ancient world for the way in which grace was supposed to operate. Aristotle, a philosopher from the fourth century B.C.E., advises the giver not to give in exchange for anything nor to seek any advantage except the advantage of the recipient (*Rhetoric* 2.7.1). The person who gives aid in the hope of gaining something in return is compared to a moneylender, not a gracious benefactor. Nevertheless, benefactors are frequently urged to consider carefully the character of the person to whom they are thinking of giving a gift, to seek out those who would be grateful rather than those who likely will fail to show gratitude. They are not to calculate this gratitude, of course, in terms of gifts they are likely to receive in return, but rather in terms of the attitude of the recipient's heart. A virtuous person of very poor means who will honor the giver and remain loyal to him or her is a far better recipient of favor than a wealthy person who may return the favor with an equally or more valuable gift but not value the relationship. The Latin author Seneca, however, recognized that favor initiated a relationship—it was not ultimately dependent on the virtue of the recipient, but on the desire and generosity of the giver.

The recipient of a favor, on the other side of this dance, understood that accepting a favor or gift involved also accepting an obligation to the giver. Favor must give birth to favor, gift to grateful response. An image developed in the ancient world to capture this ethic of reciprocity was that of three goddesses, called "the three Graces," dancing hand in hand in a circle. Seneca explains that the three goddesses represent the three aspects of gift exchange: "There is one for bestowing a benefit, one for receiving it, and a third for returning it." The three dance in a circle "for the reason that a benefit passing in its course from hand to hand returns nevertheless to the giver; the beauty of the whole is destroyed if the course is anywhere broken, and it has most beauty if it is continuous and maintains an uninterrupted succession" (Seneca, *Ben.* 1.3.2–4)

Failure to respond with gratitude marred the beauty of a social institution that was considered necessary to the survival of society and, indeed, necessary to the survival of individuals and families, who would often require aid at some point to avert some dire peril. Unlike the contractual agreement, in which each party's obligations were carefully outlined, the relationships between patrons and clients, or between friends, was not so regulated: Both parties knew only that, once initiated, the two would continue to be bound to each other. Lest this be seen as strictly a Greek or Roman mind-set, one should remember that the psalmist also well understands this ethos as he exclaims, "What shall I give back to the Lord for all his gifts to me?" (Ps. 116:12, au. trans.), and then proceeds to list the things that lie within his power to do to show his gratitude to God.

That the Greek speaker could denote both favor and gratitude, both gift and response, with the single word *charis* tells us something about the intimate relationship of giving and responding in the Classical and Greco-Roman world. Keeping this ethic in the backs of our minds will also help us understand how the authors of the New Testament understood discipleship and a life of Christian service to flow quite naturally and necessarily from the receiving of God's gifts and promises for the future.

The Content of God's Favor

As one moves through the New Testament, one encounters several different approaches to articulating the content and significance of this new outpouring of God's favor. A common thread, however, has to do with God's offer of mercy and restoration to the sinner (Mt. 1:21; 10:28; 26:28–29; Lk. 15; 19:10; Jn. 3:16–17; 12:47; 1 Tim. 1:15), the person who has abused God's gifts and kindness in the past by ignoring God's claim on that person's obedience and reverence.

All humanity begins life in God's debt, because God is the source and sustainer of all life (Acts 14:15; 17:24–25; Rev. 4:11). Because of this, no one can ever lay claim to having obligated God. As Paul wrote, "'Who has given a gift to God, to receive a gift in return?' For from God and through God and to God are all things" (Rom. 11:35–36). Despite owing God a debt of gratitude as well as having the responsibility to honor God, to be loyal to God, and to offer God the service for which God calls (that is, to obey God), humanity has largely neglected this obligation and has even chosen to live in a way that repays God with insult and affront. This is a major topic of the first three chapters of Paul's letter to the Roman Christians, in which he reproaches the Gentile for failing to honor the Creator (giving to lifeless idols the gratitude due the One God) and the Jew for failing to obey the commandments of the God who had personally revealed God's Self to Israel. In offering insult and refusing obedience to their Benefactor, all humanity thus provokes God to wrath and stands in expectation of destruction. It is God's prerogative, in other words, to assert God's honor by exterminating the ungrateful—those who have received their very life and breath from God but fail or refuse to "give God glory" (Rev. 14:6–7).

The new word about God's favor begins at this point. Rather than respond to humankind as their offenses and offensiveness merit, God provides the means by which to reverse the state of human alienation from God. The good news at the core of the New Testament message is, first, God's pardon for past offenses. Often this is expressed as forgiveness of sins (see Acts 10:43; Eph. 1:7; 2:3–10; Col. 2:13–14; Heb. 1:3; 9:14; 10:14–17), "redemption" (Rom. 3:24; Eph. 1:7), or "reconciliation" (2 Cor. 5:17–21). Frequently, the language of forgiveness or pardon is couched in terms that are in keeping with the apocalyptic worldview within which Christianity took shape. According to this worldview (see chap. 4), the present time is a period of sin that will soon end when God comes to judge the world and let loose God's wrath on all evil and disobedience. God's intervention to judge will usher in a new age in which righteousness and justice will be perfected. Thus, Paul speaks of rescue from "the present evil age" (Gal. 1:4) and from "the wrath that is coming" (1 Thess. 1:10), focusing on the aspect of being spared the expected consequences of rebellion against the Creator. Similarly, 2 Timothy 1:9–10 speaks of God's gift of deliverance from death and entrance into life and immortality. Many of these images are held together in Colossians 1:13–14: "God has rescued us from the power of darkness and transferred us into the kingdom of God's beloved Son, in whom we have redemption, the forgiveness of sins."

The good news is not only about the erasure of past offenses and God's setting aside of wrath; it is, more positively, the restoration of people to God's favor. Rather than waiting for people to come around and seek pardon, make amends and reparations, and petition God to look with favor on them once more, God has taken the initiative and invited all to step out of the shadow of alienation and into the light of God's kindness and generosity. The early Christians especially prized God's gift of the Holy Spirit (Acts 2:38; 10:45; 11:17), at once regarded as both a key gift from God and a sign of God's favor resting on the community of believers. In the Acts narrative, in fact, the giving of the Holy Spirit was the positive counterpart of forgiveness of sins (see especially Acts 2:38).

For the early church, the Holy Spirit was not simply part of a creed but a veritable participant in the gathering of Christians. The reception of the message about God's favor was often accompanied by the experience of the power of God in the community's midst (1 Cor. 2:1–5; Gal. 3:1–5; Heb. 2:3–4), evidenced in ecstatic phenomena–"signs, wonders, varied miracles, and distributions of God's Spirit according to God's will" (Heb. 2:4, au. trans.). Such signs of the Spirit's presence and power at work continued to mark both the assemblies of believers (1 Cor. 12 and 14) and the inward experience of Christians (Rom. 8:4–9; 1 Cor. 2:11–12; Gal. 4:6–7). This experience became a focal point for understanding the nature and extent of the favor of God in which the Christian stood.

Reception of the Holy Spirit was interpreted as a signal that the believer was accepted by God as part of God's family. Hence, the Spirit is called the "spirit of adoption" (Rom. 8:15–17; see Gal. 4:6–7). The experience of the Spirit became the proof, therefore, of a great favor indeed: God's incorporation of the Christians into God's own household. They were not merely pardoned offenders, then, but were received as loved children (Jn. 1:12–13; Eph. 1:5; Heb. 2:11–13). People shared in the honor of the head of their family. Reception into God's family meant a tremendous grant of honor, as believers came to be associated with the highest and most honorable "head of the household" in the cosmos.

Another image of belonging to God that appears alongside household or family imagery is the imagery of the kingdom of priests drawn from Exodus 19:5–6, God's description of Israel as God's "treasured possession," a "priestly kingdom" and "holy nation." The priest was a person set apart from his peers for special access and service to God. When this image was applied to Israel, it denoted their own favored status in God's sight above the rest of the nations. John applies this language to the worldwide community of Christians: "By your blood you ransomed for God saints from every tribe and language and people and nation; you have made them to be a kingdom and priests serving our God" (Rev. 5:9–10; see also 1:5–6). The author of 1 Peter also takes the language of Exodus 19:5–6, applying it now to the favored status God has granted to those who received the gift of pardon through Jesus. In the images of both "household" and "priesthood," the emphasis is on the privilege God has granted to believers, namely, close association with the holy God, free access to God, and an abiding place in God's favor.

Understanding God's favor to manifest itself in adoption of believers into a new family had important implications for the Christian's relationship to his or her former way of life and social connectedness. The author of 1 Peter brings these out most dramatically:

> By his great mercy he has given us a new birth into a living hope through the resurrection of Jesus Christ from the dead, and into an inheritance that is imperishable, undefiled, and unfading, kept in heaven for you, who are being protected by the power of God through faith for a salvation ready to be revealed in the last time…You know that you were ransomed from the futile ways inherited from your ancestors…You have been born anew, not of perishable but of imperishable seed. (1 Pet. 1:3–5, 18, 23)

This passage contrasts a new "inheritance" with the "inheritance" that a person acquires through his or her natural birth into a natural kinship group—an inheritance here conceived mainly as a way of life and a view of reality, both of which alienated one from knowing the One God. Much of the literature of the New Testament is dedicated to helping believers to identify and eliminate the lingering, unhealthy aspects of their first heritage and to embody the understanding of reality and patterns of behavior characteristic of their new family, God's family (in which, once again, the children must learn to resemble the Parent; see chapter 2). There is also a value judgment consistently brought to bear on this point: The way of life learned from non-Christian sources is of limited, if any, value because it leads only to decay and death, whereas the birth one has received from God opens one up to an unending life in the heavenly realm. As this value judgment was continually reinforced in the early church, individual believers were more and more apt to distance themselves from the priorities and behaviors they learned from the non-Christian society and to seek to identify themselves more fully with their emerging identity as children of God.

In this journey toward leaving behind the "futile ways" learned apart from Christ and learning a better way, the Holy Spirit again emerges as a critical resource provided by God for the believer. Paul points throughout his letters to the Spirit's leading as a reliable and, ultimately, feasible path to attaining a virtuous life. In Galatians 5:13–25, for example, Paul takes up the familiar theme of Greco-Roman ethics, namely, the struggle to rise above the domination of the passions of the flesh so that one can attain a life of virtue. Greek and Roman ethicists recognized that one's own desires (such as the desire for money, sex, or food), one's emotional responses (such as anger or fear), and physical sensations themselves (whether pleasurable or painful) could divert one from pursuing a course of action that was in line with what was noble and virtuous (see the characterization of the pre-Christian life in Eph. 2:3). Some Jewish authors, such as Philo or the writer of 4 Maccabees, regarded the Jewish Law (Torah) as God's prescription for the disease of being mastered by passions. Paul, however, pointed to God's gift of the Holy Spirit as the remedy for being led astray by passions: "Walk in line with the Spirit, and you will certainly not fulfill the desires of the flesh" (Gal. 5:16, au. trans.). Following the Spirit becomes the way in which the believer can lead a life approved by God and come in line with God's standards, quite apart from trying to follow the prescriptions of the Torah (see also Rom. 6:12–14; 8:1–14).

Paul frequently contrasts the Torah with the Spirit, portraying them as two paths by which one might seek to please God by living a righteous life (Rom. 8:1–4; 2 Cor. 3:7–18). Unlike his Jewish contemporaries, Paul found the Torah to be insufficient in terms of enabling virtue, whereas the Spirit was a living and active presence able to empower believers to live virtuous lives. Moreover, Paul regarded the Spirit's reflection of God's character and standards to be superior to that of even the Torah: It seemed to him useless to apply oneself to the pattern articulated in the Law when one could instead apply oneself to the pattern of the character of the One who gave the Law and the pattern of Jesus, who reflected the Father's character with complete precision.

John also emphasizes the importance of God's gift of the Holy Spirit, not only for birth into God's family (Jn. 3:3–8) but also for discovering and doing what pleases God. It is the Spirit that God will send after Jesus' ascension who will be the teacher of the disciples, their guide "into all truth" (Jn. 14:26; 16:13–14). By providing the Holy Spirit for believers, then, God has also provided all that is needful for a virtuous life and entry into God's kingdom (to borrow a phrase from 2 Pet. 1:3–11). It is important for the reader to mark this connection between the believer's pursuit of virtue and the resource of the Holy Spirit. The favor of God supplies not only forgiveness but the means by which the recipient of pardon may "walk in newness of life" (Rom. 6:4) in a way that pleases the Heavenly Parent.

God's favor is not exhausted by pardon, birth into God's own family, and the resources for living an honorable, virtuous life. The New Testament authors also look ahead to gifts that God will grant the people of God in the future. This will be explored more fully in chapter 4. For now, in keeping with the motif of a new birth, we can focus briefly on the subtheme of the believers' inheritance. Through being united with Jesus, the "seed" of Abraham, Christians have come into the inheritance promised to Abraham (Gal. 3:15–16, 26–29; 4:21–31, which in the early church is taken not as the promise merely of the land of Canaan but of an eternal homeland (Phil. 3:21;

Heb. 11:11–16; 13:13–14). This expansion is possible because the believers are not merely heirs of Abraham, but heirs of God (Rom. 8:17) destined to inherit the kingdom of God (Mt. 25:34; 1 Cor. 6:9–11; 15:50; Gal. 5:21). Once again, the Holy Spirit emerges prominently in connection with this future gift of God. The Spirit is seen as the "down payment" or "first installment" or "pledge" that God has given to believers, assuring them of the full inheritance promised them, toward which they are moving forward in trust (2 Cor. 1:22; 5:5; Eph. 1:13–14). This inheritance comes at the end of the present age, often being linked to the second coming of Christ (Heb. 9:26–28) and including images of sharing the glory into which Jesus, as senior brother in the family of God, has already entered (Heb. 2:9; Rev. 2:26–28).

An especially important aspect of God's favor for the early church was the assurance of God's ongoing availability to help and to give aid and resources when needed to help the church persevere. The believer faced a variety of pressures from natural kin, peers, and society. Frequently, non-Christians would become suspicious of a neighbor who joined the Christian movement. As the Gentile (i.e., non-Jewish) Christians pulled away from the worship of idols that surrounded so many aspects of Greco-Roman society, they would come to be viewed as irreverent, antisocial, and even potentially subversive. As Jewish Christians joined themselves to this new community, their Jewish peers would often object to their relaxation of strict observance of the Torah, not to mention their proclamation of a sinner and deceiver as God's Anointed One. Therefore, pressure often was brought to bear on Christians to leave their new commitments and to return to the way of life that gave neighbors assurance of their reliability, virtue, and solidarity with them.

In the face of such pressures, the believer was not left on his or her own to pursue the inheritance promised by God. Matthew and Luke both preserve teachings of Jesus about prayer, regarded here as petitions for aid addressed to God. Matthew 6 has a special emphasis on God's gifts of food and clothing, forgiveness, and rescue from trial (Mt. 6:5–15, 25–33), notably in the context of waiting and watching for God's kingdom and striving after righteousness. Jesus presents God as the archetype of the good father: "If you then, who are evil, know how to give good gifts to your children, how much more will your Father in heaven give good things to those who ask him!" (Mt. 7:11; see 7:7–11). In Luke's account of the same teaching, the Holy Spirit is singled out as the "good gift" that God gives to those who ask (Lk. 11:9–13), and elsewhere (18:1–8) Luke underscores God's commitment to bringing justice to those who call out to him: "Will not God grant justice to his chosen ones who cry to him day and night?" (18:7). John's account of Jesus' farewell discourse to his disciples (Jn. 13–17) contains repeated assurances that the disciples' prayers will be granted them, whether by Jesus (after his return to the Father) or by God himself (Jn. 14:13–14; 16:23–24, 26–27; see also 1 Jn. 3:21–22; 5:14–15).

Other New Testament voices also affirm God's availability to help those of God's household. Paul advises his friends in Philippi: "In everything by prayer and supplication with thanksgiving let your requests be made known to God" (4:6). The Pauline letters are replete with requests for prayer for God's help and notices of how God has answered such prayers (Rom. 15:30–32; 2 Cor. 1:10–11; 9:14; Eph. 2:16–19; 6:18–20; Phil. 1:9–11, 19; Col. 4:2–4; 1 Thess. 5:25; 2 Thess. 3:1–2; see also Heb. 13:18). In these passages, we find the author requesting specific prayers that God will provide deliverance for the ministry team, open up opportunities for proclaiming the good news of God's favor in Jesus, and equip the messengers to proclaim that message boldly and effectively. We also find the authors revealing the content of their prayers for the Christians addressed in the texts. Such an atmosphere suggests the importance of the conviction that God would continue to give aid both for the growth of the movement and for the maturation of disciples.

The author of the letter to the Hebrews, writing to Christians whose neighbors have long been shaming and victimizing them in order to pressure them back into conformity, is especially intent on drawing the congregation's gaze away from their besetting troubles and toward the resources that God can provide to sustain them in their contest: "Since, then, we have a great high priest who has passed through the heavens, Jesus, the Son of God, let us hold fast to our confession...Let us therefore approach the throne of grace with boldness, so that we may receive mercy and find grace to help in time of need" (Heb. 4:14, 16). Near the close of his written sermon, the author reaffirms God's nearness to help with a quotation from the Hebrew Scriptures: "he has said, 'I will never leave you or forsake you.' So we can say with confidence, 'The Lord is my helper; I will not be afraid. What can anyone do to me?'" (13:5–6). The believers were thus to carry about with them a lively sense of God's nearness and willingness to help them as they encountered difficulties walking in loyalty and obedience to God. For example, rather than allowing the poverty inflicted on them by their non-Christian neighbors to drive them away from their commitment to the God of Jesus Christ, they were encouraged to run to the God whose favor sheltered them and to seek assistance in prayer. As we will see in chapter 3, the family of God itself would become an important vehicle by which God could answer such prayers for relief or encouragement.

In this survey of how the early Christians conceptualized the specific content of the "favor of God," we have underscored the gift of the Holy Spirit not because this was seen as the single most important gift, but because the common experience of the Spirit made the Spirit a helpful focal point by which the whole constellation of God's favors and promised gifts could be held together. God's pardon and acceptance of the forgiven sinner into God's favor are signaled by the generous gift of the Spirit. This same Spirit provides proof that the believers have been made "children of God" and thus have entered a new and more honorable family. The Spirit equips and guides the believers to reflect the righteous character of the head of that family. Finally, the Spirit is seen as but the first installment of the great favors of God yet to come at the end of the age, when God's kingdom arrives in all its fullness. Along that road, the believers continue to enjoy God's favor for timely help, so that they indeed will have the resources they need to persevere in loyalty all the way to the end of their journey.

The Direction of God's Favor

The surprising aspect of God's favor is not that it is undeserved or that it cannot be earned. All favor, whether that of the emperor, the local governor, or the rich person down the street, is given, not earned, generously bestowed, not something due the recipient. The surprising aspect of God's favor is the direction in which God lavishes it throughout the New Testament, constantly overturning human norms and expectations about the boundaries of favor.

Most surprising is God's determination to extend favor to those who have made themselves enemies of God. In Romans 1–2, Paul describes this state of enmity as arising from the fact that Gentiles on the one hand, have taken the honor due God and given it to idols (seen in Jewish eyes as demon worship; see Deut. 32:17; 1 Cor. 10:19–21) and Jews, on the other hand, have flouted God's Torah: "Rarely will anyone die for a righteous person–though perhaps for a good person someone might actually dare to die. But God proves his love for us in that while we still were sinners Christ died for us...While we were enemies, we were reconciled to God through the death of his Son" (Rom. 5:7–11). The Greco-Roman culture fostered the desire to benefit friends (or those who could be made friends) and to hurt one's enemies. Typical is the advice of Isocrates: "Consider it equally disgraceful to be outdone by your enemies in doing injury and to be surpassed by your friends in doing kindness" (*To Demonicus* 26). God's favor overturns this popular logic by outdoing his enemies' injuries with kindness (something that then becomes a necessary characteristic for recipients of God's favor to imitate): "Where sin increased, grace abounded all the more" (Rom. 5:20). The New Testament abounds in declarations of the sinner as the one whom God would reach and transform by God's love and generosity (see Lk. 15; 1 Tim. 1:15; Titus 3:3–7).

There is also an emphasis on God's desire to benefit the poor and the unempowered. This is certainly learned from the Hebrew Scriptures, which celebrate God as the protector and champion of the poor, the widow, the orphan–in short, those who lack means and networks of human protection. Thus, Mary, on learning what God is about to do through the child that would be born to her, exclaims, "He has scattered the proud in the thoughts of their hearts. He has brought down the powerful from their thrones, and lifted up the lowly; he has filled the hungry with good things, and sent the rich away empty" (Lk. 1:51–53).

Paul also sees in the formation of the church itself God's selection of those who might be accounted "losers" in the eyes of society to be the special recipients of God's gifts:

> Consider your own call, brothers and sisters: not many of you were wise by human standards, not many were powerful, not many were of noble birth. But God chose what is foolish in the world to shame the wise; God chose what is weak in the world to shame the strong; God chose what is low and despised in the world, things that are not, to reduce to nothing things that are, so that no one might boast in the presence of God. (1 Cor. 1:26–29)

The church is thus kept aware that it is a community that exists wholly because of God's favor. On the one hand, this has the potential to liberate the members of the community from competitive boasting, from trying to establish the sort of internal hierarchies that divide God's family. On the other, it enables the community to understand the depths of its obligation to God, to feel the full force of the gratitude God's favor should awaken, and to regard their investment of their full selves and resources in the pursuit of discipleship and the sustaining of the community of faith as but a response to God's favor rather than as something that ought to give them influence and power over others within the community.

God's Faithfulness to Jew and Gentile

While declaring a new outpouring of God's favor, the leaders of the early church were deeply committed to setting their experience of God's favor in the context of God's faithfulness to God's earlier promises recorded in the Hebrew Scriptures. By developing connections between God's promises to Abraham and David, other selected passages from the Hebrew Scriptures that encapsulate God's promises, and the gifts of God celebrated by the early church, the Christian leaders presented the church's experience of God's favor as the working out and consummation of God's long history of dealing generously with humanity, specifically with the descendants of Abraham, Isaac, and Jacob.

The gospels are especially attuned to the importance of legitimating the early church's trust in Jesus and its experience of God through the Spirit by building up these connections with the revered oracles of God. Jesus is presented at the start of Matthew's gospel as "the son of David, the son of Abraham" (Mt. 1:1), and the genealogy that follows is crafted to place Abraham (the beginning of Israel's story), David (the high point of Israel, "the good old days" of the Hebrew Scriptures), the exile of the Judeans to Babylon (the lowest point in Israelite history), and the coming of Jesus at equally spaced intervals. This impression of equal periods of time gives a sense of God's ordering of events and God's decision at the right time to introduce Jesus, who, as son of David and son of Abraham, is a legitimate heir to the promises given to both: to David, that an heir of his would receive divine sonship and an eternal throne (2 Sam. 7:13–16); to Abraham, that in his offspring all the nations would receive God's favor (Gen. 12:3).

The early chapters of Luke's gospel also devote considerable attention to making this connection between the birth of Jesus and the promises made to Abraham and David. The angel Gabriel, announcing Jesus' conception to Mary, connects his announcement with the promises given to David of a perpetual kingdom under a descendant of David: "He will be great, and will be called the Son of the Most High, and the Lord God will give to him the throne of his ancestor David. He will reign over the house of Jacob forever; and of his kingdom there will be no end" (1:32–33). God's promises to Abraham (1:54–55, 72–73) and promises to David (1:32–33, 69) are pointed out as being fulfilled as the time of Jesus' birth draws near by both Mary and Zechariah in their songs of praise:

> "He has helped his servant Israel, in remembrance of his mercy, according to the promise he made to our ancestors, to Abraham and to his descendants forever." (Lk. 1:54–55)

> "Blessed be the Lord God of Israel, for he has looked favorably on his people and redeemed them. He has raised up a mighty savior for us in the house of his servant David, as he spoke through the mouth of his holy

> prophets from of old, that we would be saved from our enemies and from the hand of all who hate us. Thus he has shown the mercy promised to our ancestors, and has remembered his holy covenant, the oath that he swore to our ancestor Abraham." (Lk. 1:68–73)

The gospel writer's point is that God has indeed been faithful to all the promises God made and is reliable in every respect. The fruit of God's faithfulness is the good news of salvation provided in Jesus. The desire of all four evangelists to link specific events in Jesus' life with texts from the scriptures—a phenomenon far too extensive to survey here—also attests to the conviction held in the early church that "in Jesus all God's promises are 'Yes'" (2 Cor. 1:20, au. trans.).

Outside the gospels one finds the same conviction at work. The author of Hebrews, for example, presents the church's experience of God's forgiveness, acceptance into God's family, and hope for the future inheritance of a place in God's realm as the inauguration of the "new covenant" promised in Jeremiah 31:31–34 (see Heb. 8:6–13; 10:15–18). The author of 1 Peter similarly regards all the Hebrew prophets as looking ahead to the "favor" that would be shown the believers in Christ (1 Pet. 1:10–12).

One reason that so much of the New Testament addresses the continuity between God's favor and promises of old and the experience of God's favor in the church is the apparent discontinuity between Israel and the people who gathered together in the house churches. The latter group soon came to be largely Gentile (i.e., non-Israelite, non-Jewish) and did not live according to the Jewish way of life prescribed by Torah and centuries of traditional accretions to Torah, while the majority of ethnic Jews refused the message about God's favor poured out in Jesus. It was important in such an environment to demonstrate how God had in fact remained faithful to the promises given in the Hebrew Scriptures, even while the majority of the readers of those scriptures failed to join themselves to the new people of promise.

One way in which early church leaders met this challenge was by tying in the church's story with the "remnant" theme so well attested in the Old Testament. The author of Acts expresses this rather succinctly. In the midst of a sermon (Acts 3:12–26, the whole of which is well worth reading from the point of view of building or affirming connections with the Old Testament), Peter quotes the following verses from Deuteronomy 18: "Moses said, 'The Lord your God will raise up for you from your own people a prophet like me. You must listen to whatever he tells you. And it will be that everyone who does not listen to that prophet will be utterly rooted out of the people'" (Acts 3:22–23). Just as Israel itself was defined from the beginning in terms of who was faithful and who was not faithful to God's covenant and God's prophets, so, the author of Acts affirmed, it continued to be in the present time. Whoever listened to this Jesus (i.e., followed and obeyed him) would be part of Israel, but whoever refused Jesus would cease to be part of Israel. Paul uses this remnant theme far more extensively in Romans 9–11 (see 9:1–11; 11:1–5, 11–24). The Christian Jews, however few, prove God's faithfulness to Israel. Onto this core stock can be grafted people from every nation, who are thus joined to the people of God's promise. As the notion of who constitutes the "descendants of Abraham" comes to be redefined in the early church (Gal. 3:6–29; 4:21–31; see chapter 3 below), so also the continuity between God's promises in the Old Testament and the sense of God's favor at work in the church is made more apparent.

The New Testament authors, however, have no desire to downplay the expanded scope of God's favor. In the fulfillment of God's earlier promises lies a new reaching out on God's part, breaking beyond the boundaries of those who are genealogically related to Abraham. The Old Testament theme of universalism comes to full fruition here. According to the early church's teachings Jesus' ministry had been primarily to Jews. This was again understood as a sign of God's faithfulness to Israel: "Christ has become a servant of the circumcised on behalf of the truth of God in order that he might confirm the promises given to the patriarchs" (Rom. 15:8; see also Gal. 4:4–5). Nevertheless, Jesus was also remembered as reaching out to Gentiles and even as declaring that God's favor was soon to be extended to all people. The trust displayed by the centurion who sought healing for his servant from Jesus elicited Jesus' prediction that "many will come from east and west and will eat with Abraham and Isaac and Jacob in the kingdom of heaven" (Mt. 8:11). It is after Jesus' ministry to Israel is complete that he sends his disciples out to "all the nations," to tell them of God's favor and make disciples of them (Mt. 28:18–20).

The story of Acts is very much a story of the universal scope of God's favor, encompassing both the theme of God's faithfulness to his historic people, Israel, and of God's graciousness to all people. The prophecy of Amos 9:11–12 (as it was translated into the Greek version of the Hebrew Scriptures, called the Septuagint) becomes programmatic for all of Acts: "'After this I will return, and I will rebuild the dwelling of David, which has fallen; from its ruins I will rebuild it, and I will set it up, so that all other peoples may seek the Lord—even all the Gentiles over whom my name has been called. Thus says the Lord, who has been making these things known from long ago'" (Acts 15:16–18). The building up of the community of disciples of Jesus throughout Judea and Samaria is understood as the restoration of David's house. Noteworthy is the dynamic at work in this step: The restoration of "Israel" (that is, as Jewish-Christian community) happens precisely so that God's universal intent to bring all nations back to God's Self may be fulfilled at last.

It was necessary that the early church conceive of its mission as universal in scope: God's very oneness demanded that God be God to both Jews and Gentiles (see Rom 3:29–30). The Gentile nations, also God's creation (Acts 14:15–17; 17:22–31), could not be left outside the scope of God's favor, with the result that pardon for offenses against God, adoption into God's family, and the promise of the inheritance given to Abraham came also to the Gentile who responded to God's favor with trust and gratitude. Once again, the importance of the Holy Spirit for the early church's understanding of God's favor comes to the fore, because it is precisely the Gentile's reception of the same Spirit that becomes the proof that God "has given even to the Gentiles the repentance that leads to life" (Acts 11:18; see Acts 10–11; 15). The most fully developed expression of the universal scope of God's favor is Ephesians 1–3.

Jesus—the Mediator of God's Favor

A second distinctive aspect of God's favor in the New Testament is the way in which it enters the human scene, namely through the life, death, and resurrection of Jesus of Nazareth. Jesus is the focal point, the lens through which the light of God's favor and promises come into focus and shine out on humanity (Jn. 1:17–18; 3:16–17; 14:6; 2 Cor. 1:20; Eph. 1:6; Col. 1:19–20). One word that stands out in the discussion of Jesus' role in securing God's favor is *mediator:* "There is one God; there is also one mediator between God and humankind, Christ Jesus, himself human, who gave himself a ransom for all" (1 Tim. 2:5–6). The author of the letter to the Hebrews uses the language of priesthood, priests being understood as those who stood in God's presence on behalf of human beings (Heb. 5:1) in a capacity that allowed them to repair relationships injured by human affront or to secure divine favor: "Since, then, we have a great high priest who has passed through the heavens, Jesus, the Son of God,...let us therefore approach the throne of favor with boldness, so that we may receive mercy and find favor to help in time of need" (Heb. 4:14, 16, NRSV modified). This author also uses the term *mediator* to describe Jesus (Heb. 8:6; 9:15; 12:24).

Jesus is thus cast rather prominently in the role of "broker," that is, as a person whose principal gift is access to the favor of another Patron. The mediator creates a relationship where previously none existed (or, in this case, where enmity and alienation existed). For Jesus, this means not merely the introduction of the believer into God's court, as a Roman governor might have pleasantly sent a protege to the emperor with a warm letter of recommendation. Rather, Jesus' brokerage is much more complicated. He is presented in the gospels as the One through whom divine favors flow out to human beings in need. He is also responsible for removing the enmity that previously existed between sinful humans, who affronted and provoked God's wrath at every turn, and the repulsed Deity. Beyond even this, however, it is Jesus who is credited with leading his followers into a full enjoyment of God's favor and God's willingness to provide them with all the benefits previously listed. Jesus' death becomes prominent in New Testament discussions of how he effects this mediation.

Throughout the four gospels, Jesus is seen as the channel of God's favor through his acts of healing and other such miracles that bring needed aid to people. This aspect of God's favor is so prominent in the gospels that it cannot here be surveyed in any degree of completeness, so we will restrict our discussion to a few passages. As Jesus steps onto the scene of his public ministry in the gospels, he begins not only by declaring that God's kingdom has drawn near but also by dispensing the favors of the Divine King whose reign has come. In Luke's presentation of Jesus' ministry, the giving of sight to the blind and liberation of the oppressed (e.g., the demon-possessed and the crippled, not to understate the social and political implications of Jesus' call) are integral parts of the "year of the Lord's favor" that he proclaims (Lk. 4:16–21).

The reader of Matthew, Mark, and Luke should be struck by the evangelists' interest in Jesus' growing reputation as a healer and exorcist (see, for example, Lk. 6:17–18). People come to him from the whole of Palestine, hoping to receive what they have no doubt been praying for over a long span of time. Even a Roman centurion, a member of the occupying force in Judea (although one who was himself a benefactor of the Jewish people), hears of the kinds of favor that Jesus could provide and sends friends to him to request healing for his servant. Witnesses to (or recipients of) Jesus' gifts of wholeness are aware that God is ultimately the source of these benefits, Jesus being the mediator through whom divine favors are being lavished on the people (see Lk. 5:25–26; 7:16; 8:39; 9:43; 17:15, 18; Jn. 3:2).

One particularly poignant episode occurs early in the synoptic gospels (that is, in Matthew, Mark, and Luke–called "synoptic" because they all write from a rather similar perspective). Four men take great pains to get their paralyzed friend close to Jesus while he is teaching the people in a crowded house. Jesus, observing their trust in his ability to supply what this man needs, declares the man's sins to be pardoned. This invites considerable debate:

> Some of the scribes said to themselves, "This man is blaspheming." But Jesus, perceiving their thoughts, said, "Why do you think evil in your hearts? For which is easier, to say, 'Your sins are forgiven,' or to say, 'Stand

> up and walk'? But so that you may know that the Son of Man has authority on earth to forgive sins"—he then said to the paralytic—"Stand up, take your bed and go to your home." (Mt. 9:3–6)

The scribes are correct to think that only God can pardon offenses committed against God, but Jesus will demonstrate that, just as he has been given God's authority to grant divine favor (i.e., healing), so also he has been given authority to give other benefits on God's behalf (namely, pardon). The whole of Jesus' public career can be summarized by Peter in Acts with the term *euergesia*, "well doing," a term frequently used to speak of benefactors who gave generously to the public (as in Acts 10:37–38). Through this Jesus, God's favors come to people in an extraordinary, immediate, and quite personal manner.

Although they were indeed interested in Jesus' miracles and other acts of opening up people to God's beneficence, the early Christians were most concerned with Jesus' death as the focal point by which God's favor broke out into the human realm. The "cross"—the fact that Jesus died a shameful death, being executed as a criminal in the most degrading manner possible—was indeed a "stumbling block" that kept many from responding positively to the Christian message (1 Cor. 1:23). If people understood that this death was endured "for us," however, it would be seen no longer as a disgrace but, rather, as a beneficent act that, together with Jesus' resurrection and ascension, secures God's favor for humanity and ratifies the new covenant. The simple, repeated declaration that Jesus "gave himself," or died "for us," "for many," "for me," "for you" in the New Testament serves as a constant reminder of the favor shown at the cross (Mt. 20:28; Lk. 22:19; Jn. 6:51; 11:49–52; Rom. 5:8; 2 Cor. 5:14–15; Gal. 1:4; 2:20; Eph. 5:2, 25; 1 Thess. 5:10; 1 Tim. 2:6; Titus 2:14).

The concept of the "noble death" was indeed central to the early church's attempts to make sense out of a Messiah who was crucified, but whom God raised up to life. Orators and poets lauded the person who died voluntarily in a manner that exemplified virtue (usually courage) and in a manner that brought benefit to others. How can an execution be a voluntary death?

The gospel writers, especially, emphasize that the crucifixion is something Jesus voluntarily endures. The fact that Jesus three times tells his disciples what will befall him in Jerusalem shows that he "saw it coming," and goes forward anyway–that is, he voluntarily accepts the fact that he will be nailed to a cross, even though he can easily avoid this end (see Mt. 16:21–23; 17:9–12, 22–23; 20:17–19). Jesus' prayer in Gethsemane further reinforces the impression that Jesus voluntarily accepts the death that lies before him (Mt. 26:36–44). Additionally, that prayer shows Jesus' death to be a death endured in the pursuit of virtue. Here, that virtue is obedience to God (a death endured out of regard for God's right to order our lives and command our service). The prayer in Gethsemane also begins to link Jesus' death with God's favor, because it is by means of enduring the cross that Jesus allows God's will for humanity to be done. Finally, Matthew underscores the voluntary nature of Jesus' death in Jesus' exclamation that he could order twelve legions of angels to fight for him against the arresting soldiers, but refrains (Mt. 26:53–54). One may also scan John's gospel for similar signs of interest in presenting the cross as Jesus' voluntary offering of his life, even going so far as to dispatch Judas to carry out the betrayal (Jn. 10:17–18; 13:18–19, 21–30).

The main focus of New Testament authors is, however, Jesus' endurance of the cross as a noble display of beneficence–an act embraced by the benefactor who gave his all to bring benefit to others. The fact that the act required Jesus' enduring pain and shame only heightens the believer's appreciation for the kindness and generosity that led Jesus to embrace such hardship for the sake of his clients. This death was a manifestation not just of Jesus' favor, but also of God's favor: It is "by the favorable disposition of God" that Jesus "tastes death on behalf of all people" (Heb. 2:9, au. trans.). Jesus' death thus comes to be seen less and less as an act of the Roman government than as the provision set forward out of God's own kindness toward humanity to bring back all people to God's favor (see Rom. 8:32). The emphasis throughout the New Testament on the fulfillment of Old Testament prophecies in the trial, death, and resurrection of Jesus (see the summary statements in Lk. 24:25–27, 44–47, which are also developed elsewhere in the gospels) expresses the conviction that the cross was God's provision from ages past for the restoration of Israel and the extending of favor to all nations.

The early Christians explored many avenues as they reflected on how such a death could benefit others. The author of Hebrews, for example, contemplates Jesus' death as a contest in which Jesus engages the enemy of humanity to liberate them: "Since, therefore, the children share flesh and blood, he himself likewise shared the same things, so that through death he might destroy the one who has the power of death, that is, the devil, and free those who all their lives were held in slavery by the fear of death" (Heb. 2:14–15). This parallels the interpretation of Socrates' death by philosophers, such as Seneca, who held that Socrates refused to flee execution when given the chance so that he might "free humankind from the fear of...death and imprisonment" (*Moral Epistles* 24.4), although with the added emphasis now on the defeat of the personal mind behind evil, namely Satan (see chapter 4).

Jesus is thus presented as the liberator of humankind, a person who died in order to make slaves (metaphorically speaking) into free persons, emancipation from slavery being considered a very great favor. This leads into the more common tendency to interpret Jesus' death using the language of ransom or redemption ("buying back"). Jesus suffers death, according to this line of thought, as the "exchange price" for buying back those who have enslaved themselves (or been enslaved) to sin and for restoring them to favor and a privileged position in the household of God. Jesus speaks of his own death as "a ransom for many" (Mk. 10:45), as does the author of 1 Timothy, in whose eyes Jesus "gave himself a ransom for all" (1 Tim. 2:6). To what were human beings enslaved, that they required ransom? Apart from Jesus, people are enslaved to "sin" or "iniquity" (Gal. 1:4; Titus 2:14), that is, they have sold themselves into slavery to the passions of the flesh, to the mind alienated from God (Rom. 6:6, 12–14, 16–19). Thus, "redemption" can be presented as synonymous with "the forgiveness of sins" (Col. 1:14). Writing mainly to Gentile Christians, the author of 1 Peter describes this state of sin as the cultural inheritance of the Gentile world, the worldview and behaviors learned before encountering Jesus: "You know that you were ransomed from the futile ways inherited from your ancestors, not with perishable things like silver or gold, but with the precious blood of Christ, like that of a lamb without defect or blemish" (1 Pet. 1:18–19). Writing about himself and other Jewish Christians, Paul regards this ransom as effecting freedom from the Torah and, specifically, the "curse of the law" (Gal. 3:10–14; 4:4–5) pronounced on Israel for failing to "observe and obey all the things written in the book of the law" (Gal. 3:10). Within the matrix of an apocalyptic worldview (see chapter 4), with its stark contrast between this age and the age of God's kingdom, the ransoming of human beings means also their liberation from this present age and its dissolution; hence, Jesus "gave himself for our sins to set us free from the present evil age" (Gal. 1:4).

Ransom *from* servitude also means liberation *for* participating in a new state of being. This state of freedom includes first a life of virtue–something impossible while in bondage to sin or "under the law": "He himself bore our sins in his body on the cross, so that, free from sins, we might live for righteousness" (1 Pet. 2:24). Jesus died "in order to bring you to God" (1 Pet. 3:18), that is, to restore people to the presence and favor of God, from whom their sin and darkened minds had alienated them. John borrows language formerly used to describe Israel as a "priestly kingdom" (Exod. 19:6) in order to express the result of Jesus' ransom of people. "[Jesus] freed us from our sins by his blood, and made us to be a kingdom, priests serving his God and Father" (Rev. 1:5–6). "By your blood you ransomed for God saints from every tribe and language and people and nation; you have made them to be a kingdom and priests serving our God, and they will reign on earth" (Rev. 5:9–10). Redemption has brought to the believers a place in God's household (recall the language of adoption as sons and daughters of God), a new inheritance, and a new dignity.

Not surprisingly, given the Jewish matrix of early Christianity, this ransom or redemption is frequently presented in language and imagery taken from the sacrificial system of the Old Testament. Jesus' death is called a "sacrifice of atonement" (Rom. 3:24–25; see 1 Jn. 2:2)–now made by God on our behalf! Where Jesus is said to die "for sins," this would also recall the common Septuagint (Greek translations of the Hebrew Scriptures in wide use among diaspora Jews) designation for sin offerings, called merely "for sins." These terms recall the sacrifices brought by the Israelites and offered for them by the priests as the means of reconciliation between God and the offending human beings, as well as the climactic event of the Jewish liturgical year, the Day of Atonement (Yom Kippur), on which the high priests offered sacrifices for the sins of the whole people (see Lev. 16). The Old Testament precedent of a death, or the shedding of blood, as the effective means of reconciling God and sinner thus provides an important lens for viewing the death of Jesus as a beneficial act.

The author of the letter to the Hebrews goes to the greatest lengths to describe the effects of Jesus' death as a sacrifice for sins. He uses the Old Testament extensively to legitimate such an unconventional sacrifice (to put it mildly), finding in the Septuagint version of Psalm 40:6–8 the divine authorization for the setting aside of the animal sacrifices and the offering up of a "body," one specifically prepared by God (Heb. 10:1–10). Jesus' priestly act (he is both priest and victim in this ritual) closely mirrors the high priest's actions on the Day of Atonement. The high priest took the blood of a goat into the Holy of Holies, the heart of the Jerusalem temple, in order to cover or wash away the defilements mystically incurred there by the sins of the Israelites. Similarly, Jesus' ascension into heaven is taken as his entrance into the "heavenly sanctuary," the true tabernacle made by God and not human beings, to cleanse the Holy of Holies of God's real presence with his own blood. The author is applying sacrificial images quite heavily as a means of articulating the conviction that Jesus' death (and God's vindication of this Jesus as God's agent of deliverance) removed all the barriers that stood between people and God, restoring them to divine favor. The ritual imagery serves as a vehicle to convey the reality of God's promise: "I will remember their sins and their lawless deeds no more" (Jer. 31:34, as quoted in Heb. 10:17).

Just as God's favor has been seen to include past, present, and future gifts, so the specific favor of ransom or redemption remains incomplete, looking ahead to the consummation of God's kindness in the future. Liberated "from the present evil age" (Gal. 1:4), the believer has not yet entered the age that is coming but still awaits "the redemption of our bodies" in the resurrection (Rom. 8:23). Like Israel, liberated from slavery in Egypt, enjoying the dignity of being a "priestly kingdom" before God in the desert (Ex. 19:6), yet still looking ahead to the final state of occupying the land of promise, the early Christians saw themselves as living in an in-between state, enjoying God's favor but still awaiting in trust the fulfillment of God's full promise.

The authors of the New Testament thought that Jesus' mediation between human beings and God, which so characterized his life and death, had to continue after his resurrection. Paul, for example, understands Jesus as presently standing at God's right hand, interceding on behalf of the believers (Rom. 8:34), and he presents this as proof that there is no one who can condemn the believer in God's presence and that nothing can attack from without the bond of favor between God and God's people (Rom. 8:31–39). The author of Hebrews, moreover, sees Jesus' work as mediator—as broker securing God's favor for those who approach God through Jesus—as mainly taking place after Jesus' ascension to God's right hand. It is with his ascension into "heaven itself," that realm of God beyond the visible creation of heavens and earth, that Jesus can enter the heavenly sanctuary and cleanse it of the defilement (and thus the remembrance) of human sins against God (Heb. 9:23–24; 10:17). It is from the vantage point of sitting beside God that Jesus can continue to work to maintain God's favorable acceptance of the believers and thus assure the believers who continue to look to Jesus that they will arrive at the end of their pilgrimage intact: "He is able for all time to save those who approach God through him, since he always lives to make intercession for them" (Heb. 7:25; see also 1 Jn. 2:1).

Jesus is regarded in every respect as a reliable mediator of God's favor—past, present, and future. He is sympathetic toward the plight of humans struggling to be faithful (Heb. 2:16–18; 4:15), yet without any obstacles in his own relationship with the Father, such that his intercession on behalf of others is always favorably received by God (Heb. 7:26–28). His relationship with God, defined as "Son," places him closest to the heart of the head of the household that is the cosmos, and gives his clients the greatest assurance that his mediation will be successful (Heb.

3:1–6; 10:19–22). Moreover, Jesus is presented as "the same yesterday and today and forever" (Heb. 13:8), a declaration that would have been heard not so much as a proposition about Jesus' unchanging nature but about Jesus' unchanging loyalty and goodwill, his utter commitment to follow through on that with which he is entrusted by his clients.

It is quite possibly the emphasis on Jesus as mediator between humanity and God that led early Christians to put a new face, as it were, on the Jewish figure of Wisdom, God's partner and agent in creation. As the Jewish Wisdom tradition develops, Wisdom acquires a rather personal appearance: Wisdom becomes not just some ideal to be pursued, but a "she," a personal coworker with God. Proverbs 8 contains a sort of self-disclosure statement by Wisdom, who presents her virtues, attributes, and benefits. Toward the end of this poem, we read: "When God established the heavens, I was there…beside him, like a master worker; and I was daily his delight, rejoicing before him always…Whoever finds me finds life and obtains favor from the LORD; but those who miss me injure themselves" (Prov. 8:27, 30, 35–36). Wisdom was God's partner in creation; Wisdom herself delights God; and, most significantly for our discussion, those who gain Wisdom enjoy God's patronage and find life.

The author of Wisdom of Solomon, a text written sometime in the first century B.C.E. or C.E., writes concerning this figure of Wisdom: "She is…a pure emanation of the glory of the Almighty…For she is a reflection of eternal light, a spotless mirror of the working of God, and an image of God's goodness" (7:25–26). Again, Wisdom stands between God and God's creation from its beginning to the present day, renewing all things (Wis. 7:27), and even sitting beside God's throne (Wis. 9:4). Moreover, Wisdom "passes into holy souls and makes them friends of God" (Wis. 7:27); that is, Wisdom acts as a broker or mediator between people and God, establishing friendship between the two.

The common ground between Wisdom and Jesus, namely in their roles as mediators between God and humanity, may have led early Christians to the insight that, in fact, the two were identical. This would explain why New Testament authors draw rather heavily on traditions about Wisdom to speak of Jesus' activity before his incarnation, as well as to express the significance of his having been made flesh (Jn. 1:14). Thus, it is the pre-Incarnate Son who now is the "image of the invisible God" (Col. 1:15) or the "reflection of God's glory and the exact imprint of God's very being" (Heb. 1:3). Just as one could look to Wisdom to see the perfect reflection of God–that is, just as one could know God through pursuing Wisdom–the New Testament authors now claim that one comes to know God through looking at Jesus. John joins perhaps most prominently in this affirmation that to look at Jesus is to look at the very face of the invisible God: "Whoever has seen me has seen the Father" (Jn. 14:9; cf. 1:18; 14:7; 15:24).

Alongside attributing to Jesus the ability to reflect God's character and essence to humanity, which was formerly attributed to Wisdom, early Christians now attributed to the Son Wisdom's role in creation and the maintenance of the cosmos: "In him all things in heaven and on earth were created, things visible and invisible...all things have been created through him and for him. He himself is before all things, and in him all things hold together" (Col. 1:16–17; see Jn. 1:3, 10). The author of Hebrews also underscores both aspects of the Son's role in creation: "Through him God also created the ages...The Son sustains all things by his powerful word" (Heb. 1:2–3, NRSV modified). The early Christians came to see in Jesus the lens through which God's favor and kindness toward creation has been manifested from beginning to end, and not just the means by which God was reconciled to an alienated humanity.

God's Favor and Freedom

One of the more important debates within the early church centered on the role that Torah, the law laid down by God for Israel, would have within the new community. The question came to the fore especially as Gentiles, who were raised "outside the law" (1 Cor. 9:21), began to respond to the message about God's favor in Jesus and to join themselves to the church. A vocal part of the constituency of the early church called for these Gentiles "to be circumcised and ordered to keep the law of Moses" (Acts 15:5; see 15:1–5). These Christians understandably thought that it was still God's expectation that the Torah be followed as the law that ruled the covenant people.

There was also considerable social pressure on Jewish Christians from non-Christian Jews to maintain the practices that set Israel apart from "the nations" (see the references to "persecution" as the motivation for the attempt by Jewish Christian missionaries to call Gentile Christians to Torah observance in Gal. 5:11; 6:12). Both parties were interested in maintaining the boundaries of Israel as the covenant people.

The most vocal opponent of this point of view was Paul, who had especially associated himself with the mission to the Gentiles (Gal. 2:7–9; Eph. 3:1–10). He sought to dissuade Gentile believers from accepting circumcision and following Torah's regulations—and to dissuade Jewish Christians from trying to pressure Gentile Christians in this direction—by formulating an essential opposition between "works of the Torah" and "God's favor," or, more commonly, "trust" (faith) in God's favor shown in Jesus (see Rom. 3:21–30; Gal. 2:15–17, 21). Paul had come to the conclusion that, ironically, the attempt to impose Torah on Gentile converts—or even the attempt to uphold Torah's boundaries between Gentile and Jew within the new community (see Gal. 2:11–14)—now amounts to resisting God rather than obeying God. Although Paul's rivals believed that they were being faithful to God (i.e., by obeying the stipulations of Torah and spreading Torah-righteousness), Paul sees these actions as a rejection of God's favor, an opposition to God's new initiative, and, ultimately, an act of distrust in Jesus, God's provision for reconciliation and, through the gift of the Spirit, for a life of righteousness.

For Paul, pardon, righteousness, and entrance into the new covenant are all gifts of God. In Romans, Paul's most mature reflection on this mystery of Jew and Gentile brought together in one church, Paul especially emphasizes God's initiative in this new pouring out of favor, granting pardon and inclusion to whomever God desires:

> Is there injustice on God's part? By no means! For he says to Moses, "I will have mercy on whom I have mercy, and I will have compassion on whom I have compassion." So it depends not on human will or exertion, but on God who shows mercy...He has mercy on whomever

> he chooses, and he hardens the heart of whomever he chooses. (Rom. 9:14–16, 18)

Using the familiar image of the potter and the clay, Paul stresses God's freedom and God's right to do as God pleases in God's dealings with humanity. Paul's experience of the risen Christ, moreover, leads him to understand that God was indeed exercising the freedom to reach out now to Jew and Gentile alike on the same basis. Just as both the Jews and Gentiles found themselves in the same plight, namely alienation from God on account of their sins (whether the sin was committed by a person "under Torah" or "outside of Torah" made no difference to the God who "shows no partiality," Rom. 2:11), so now God has extended to both the gift of pardon and righteousness. The church is composed of all

> the objects of mercy, which he has prepared beforehand for glory–including us whom he has called, not from the Jews only but also from the Gentiles. As indeed he says in Hosea, "Those who were not my people I will call 'my people,' and her who was not beloved I will call 'beloved.' And in the very place where it was said to them, 'You are not my people,' there they shall be called children of the living God." (Rom. 9:23–26)

Paul uses a text from Hosea that tells of God's initiative in pardoning and restoring the disobedient nation of Israel to speak of God's initiative in extending that same mercy to all people, whether Jew or Gentile.

This new act of favor is, according to Paul, the ultimate expression of God's righteousness–a righteousness that pardons and restores, that empowers a life of righteousness (Rom. 3:21–26). God's impartiality, an important component of justice (righteousness), means that the Jew who lives "under the law" but who nevertheless fails to live by the whole law is in no better a position than the Gentile who lives "outside the law" (Rom. 2). God has provided for both a solution that places Jew and Gentile on equal ground: The same "atoning sacrifice," namely Jesus' death, secures pardon for Jew and Gentile, even as the gift of the Holy Spirit leads both Jew and Gentile into a life of righteousness–something Torah was never able to do because of the power sin had over all humanity. The Jews who reject the divine initiative in Jesus are actually found to be in rebellion against God, "being ignorant of the righteousness that comes from God, and seeking to establish their own, they have not submitted to God's righteousness. For Christ is the end of the law so that there may be righteousness for everyone who believes" (Rom. 10:3–4). The Jewish Christians stand in God's favor, but not on the basis of Torah observance: "So too at the present time there is a remnant [from Israel], chosen by grace. But if it is by grace, it is no longer on the basis of works, otherwise grace would no longer be grace. What then? Israel failed to obtain what it was seeking. The elect obtained it, but the rest were hardened" (Rom. 11:5–7).

In order to displace Torah, Paul looks back to the precedent of Abraham, a precedent from, significantly, the period prior to the giving of the Torah to Moses. Abraham becomes the model for how God's favor breaks into the world. God again takes the initiative, giving promises to Abraham; Abraham's part is to trust God's promises, to trust that God is able and trustworthy to do as God has promised. In Abraham, moreover, Paul sees the father of the Jewish family and of the family that God has called together from Jews and Gentiles, "the father of many nations" (Rom. 4:17). It is not circumcision but trust in God's favor and the efficacy of God's gifts that is the common denominator defining who is part of this family (Rom. 4:11–12, 16).

The Torah, with its emphasis on Jews making themselves distinct from the nations around them, would have no continuing role in legislating who could be part of the people of God nor, ultimately, in regulating the lives of the people of God. Its value was now instructional, not legal. More important now was God's giving of the Holy Spirit to both Jews and Gentiles, who had received God's grant of pardon in Jesus. The people of God would no longer be marked off from the rest of humanity by the covenant markers of Judaism (such as circumcision, Sabbath observance, dietary regulations, and the like) but by possession of–or, better, possession by–the Holy Spirit (Acts 10:44–48; 11:15–18; 15:8–9; Rom. 8:9–17; Gal. 3:1–3). The ultimate warrant for not imposing Torah as the abiding rule of the early church was, then, God's freedom to have mercy on whom God desired, to extend God's favor in whatever direction God pleased, the gift of the Spirit being the indisputable evidence of this mercy and favor.

Chapter 2

Discipleship

The Way of God

The early Christians, including the New Testament authors, understood that acceptance of a gift also entailed the acceptance of an obligation to the giver. This understanding derived from the social context in which they lived, a context in which the mutual exchange of favors–reciprocity–was a core value. In the grossly unequal relationship between God and human beings, one could never "repay" the favors of God. One would, however, do what was in one's power, namely, give God all the honor, testimony, and loyal service that one could.

Such a response to God was clearly visible in the life of Abraham, a model for synagogue and church alike. Having received God's promises and experienced God's personal patronage in being taken into God's confidence, being allowed to know God's plans, and being protected by God wherever he and his family went, Abraham understood the depth of his obligation of gratitude. Wherever God called him to go, he went; whatever honor he could show God, he did; whatever service he was called on to perform, he performed, even if it meant giving up his own child (see Jas. 2:14–26). Those who hear the story of God's favors bestowed in Christ and favors promised for the future understand that similar trust and subsequent obedience is required on their part.

Several authors make explicit connections between the reception of God's favor and the necessary and suitable response of discipleship. Paul probably sets the high-water mark in 2 Corinthians: "He died for all, so that those who live might live no longer for themselves, but for him who died and was raised for them" (2 Cor. 5:15). The generosity of Jesus in giving his life for people means that a debt of gratitude has been incurred by those people—a challenge to meet favor with favor, to respond as generously to Jesus as Jesus acted toward them. Paul understands that nothing less than "living for Jesus" begins to show appropriate gratitude to one who "died for all."

The author of the letter (or, better, sermon) to the Hebrews also articulates this intimate connection between gift (or promise of gift) and grateful response: "Since we are receiving a kingdom that cannot be shaken, let us give thanks [or, show gratitude], by which we offer to God an acceptable worship with reverence and awe" (Heb. 12:28). This gratitude involves both bringing public honor to God and performing acts of love and service toward the members of God's family (Heb. 13:15–16). The author of 1 Peter also emphasizes the first of these: The result of the believers' new identity as God's "holy nation" and "special possession" (au. trans.) must be that they "proclaim the mighty acts (literally, 'virtues') of him who called you out of darkness into his marvelous light" (1 Pet. 2:9). The author of Ephesians underscores the second: The doing of "good works" is the necessary outcome of the new life God has given believers through Jesus (Eph. 2:7–10).

Paul also introduces the strange declaration in 1 Corinthians 15:10 that "[God's] grace toward me has not been in vain." In context here, Paul is speaking of the fervor and wholeheartedness with which he has engaged the missionary work to which God called him. Paul has acted nobly, responding to God's gift of bringing Paul to know Jesus and setting Paul's feet on the path to life by pouring himself out to serve this God. From this perspective, God's gifts to Paul have borne pleasant fruit for the Giver (see Heb. 6:7–8). Thus, Paul shows his awareness that favor can prove to be either well shown or shown "in vain," depending on whether or not the recipient responds nobly and gratefully (gracefully) to the kindness he or she has received. He admonishes the Corinthian Christians themselves "not to receive God's gift in vain" (2 Cor. 6:1; au. trans.). Accepting God's gift without allowing it to have its full effect in their lives and to produce the full crop of a grateful response would mean, in effect, cutting short the beautiful and salvific dance that God initiated, cutting short the relationship of favor between God and church before the most crucial benefit had been bestowed, namely, deliverance from the present age and entrance into the coming, eternal age.

Responding to God's favor–pursuing the "way of God" in discipleship–is thus an indispensable aspect of the New Testament message. The goal of this section is to outline the contours of this grateful response to God as the authors of the New Testament give it shape.

"Fulfilling the Just Requirement of the Law"

Israel had already formed a clear conception of how to respond appropriately to the God who created them and who made them into a nation that had been and would continue to be the recipient of God's special protection and favor. This response was the doing of Torah, the fulfilling of the commandments that God had laid out for them through Moses. It is important that we understand that observance of the Jewish Law was itself understood as a *response* to the experience of God's favors, not a means by which to "earn salvation." The grateful recipient of God's favors would thus seek to be diligent in the observance of these commandments, which included the laws that kept Jews clearly separate from the Gentile nations around them. Laws involving Sabbath observance, following dietary restrictions, and circumcising male children were the most prominent in this regard.

Imitation of God stands out as a prominent aspect of human response to God within the Pentateuch itself, notably the Levitical law code: "You will be holy, even as I the LORD your God am holy" (Lev. 11:44–45, au. trans.). This holiness includes mirroring God's character, as is seen in the commitment to justice in all its forms that Torah seeks to inculcate (such as honoring the life created by God or honoring vows made before God) and also God's activities and rhythms, making visible in the world the qualities of the invisible God. The Jew's commitment to resting on the Sabbath is primarily an imitation of the rhythms of the God who rested on the Sabbath day (and thus a witness to God as Creator of all; Gen. 2:2–3; Ex. 20:8–11). The Jew's care in distinguishing between what is clean and unclean (the bulk of the dietary and purity laws found in Leviticus) is a reflection of God's activity of distinguishing between what is "clean" and "unclean," seen primarily in God's choice of Israel to be God's own possession (as distinct from the many Gentile nations; Lev. 20:22–26).

Within the early church, however, it was by no means clear if this same response to God was still appropriate. Particularly as the church became a largely Gentile community, accepted by God and endowed with God's Holy Spirit apart from such "ethnic" marks as circumcision, kosher laws, and Sabbath rules, the appropriateness of identifying Torah with the grateful response that God seeks came more and more into question and was finally rejected in favor of a new construction of what response would please God. How was it possible for early Christians to regard Israel's purity codes, dietary laws, and rites, such as circumcision, as passé?

Paul's concept of the "fullness of time" (see Gal. 3:23–4:7) bears directly on this question. Prior to the coming of Jesus, it was incumbent on Israel to keep its separateness from Gentile nations so as not to become like the nations that provoked God to wrath by their idolatries and their sinful ways of life. This state of affairs was, however, a temporary measure in effect only until the time set by God for God's promises to Abraham to be fulfilled. These promises included "many nations" coming to worship the One God.

With the death and resurrection of Jesus, a new stage in God's dealings with humanity came into being in which one humanity under the One God became a possibility. In this new humanity, Jew and Gentile would be joined. The Jew would not become like the Gentile (assimilating to a lifestyle that God rejected), but neither would the Gentile become like the Jew (assimilating to a lifestyle that belonged to an age that was past, a lifestyle designed to preserve the separateness and distinctiveness of God's people until the Messiah, the "Seed" that would receive the promise, came). Instead, both would become like the Righteous One, namely Jesus, brought to life in each person by the very Spirit of God (Rom. 8:1–16; Gal. 5:13–25). The resurrection and exaltation of Jesus was interpreted as God's unique seal of approval, God's refusal to allow the Righteous One to remain under an unjust sentence of death for blasphemy and deception. The resurrection showed that Jesus did indeed reveal the way that pleased God rather than the opposite, and so the path that Jesus taught and that he himself walked came to be understood as the divinely appointed means by which people—all people—might enter God's kingdom.

The synoptic gospel writers are especially interested in preserving stories about the controversies between Jesus and other Jews concerning how to observe Torah. These stories provide, on the one hand, the interpretative keys by which Christians can relate to the Jewish Torah. These stories also display the differences between Christian and non-Christian Jewish keeping of the Torah. The criticisms leveled against Jesus reflect the kinds of criticisms that could be leveled by non-Christian Jews against Christians, but Jesus' "victory" in each controversy, combined with God's final pronouncement on Jesus in the resurrection, assures Christians that their own way of fulfilling God's just decrees is indeed the correct one.

In the church's memory of Jesus' teachings, we find that Jesus affirms a great deal of Torah, in particular the commandment regarding love for God and love for neighbor (as enacted in the second part of the Ten Commandments; see Mt. 22:34–40). Jesus' identification of love for God as the most important commandment is not surprising, because Deuteronomy 6:1–4 was recited by pious Jews twice daily and would thus have been familiar. His choice of love for neighbor as the close second is somewhat more innovative, all the more as it appears in the midst of the Levitical holiness laws. It is as if Jesus had identified love for neighbor as the central aspect of mirroring God's holiness—a conclusion that is strongly supported by the rest of Jesus' claims about the proper application of Torah (and one that would be determinative for early Christian ethos: see Rom. 13:8–10 and Gal. 5:15).

A number of the teachings of Jesus preserved by the church deal specifically with the transcending of those commands that served to maintain boundaries, both between Jews and Gentiles and within Judaism between the more rigorous observers and the "sinners" within Israel. When certain Pharisees criticize Jesus' disciples for not performing ritual washing of the hands before eating, Jesus replies by declaring to the crowd that had gathered,

> "There is nothing outside a person that by going in can defile, but the things that come out are what defile"..."Do you not see that whatever goes into a person from outside cannot defile, since it enters, not the heart but the stomach, and goes out into the sewer?" (Thus he declared all foods clean.) And he said, "It is what comes out of a person that defiles. For it is from within, from the human heart, that evil intentions come: fornication, theft, murder, adultery, avarice, wickedness, deceit, licentiousness, envy, slander, pride, folly. All these evil things come from within, and they defile a person." (Mk. 7:15, 18–23).

Jesus elevates the importance of attention to those attitudes and behaviors that poison human relations as the true source of the pollution that disqualifies one from having access to the Holy God. Perhaps Jesus was speaking hyperbolically, but his followers soon came to understand this as a divine ruling (Jesus was, after all, authorized by God to speak on God's behalf; see Mk. 9:7) rewriting the purity codes of Torah. In one bold stroke, God's representative nullifies the meaningfulness of distinguishing between clean and unclean foods, of avoiding certain people in polluting conditions (such as the leper, the hemorrhaging woman, the less-observant Jew), and of ritual purifications. In their place, a wholly ethical view of pollution and purity is erected, and the people of God are called to respond to their divine benefactor by abstaining from these particular pollutions. Mirroring God's holiness as "separateness" from the Gentile nations preserved through dietary and purity codes is replaced with mirroring God's holiness as purity of heart and separation from those attitudes and actions that pervert and inhibit human relationships.

A cluster of stories about Jesus centers on the keeping of the Sabbath. Although no story shows Jesus making a sweeping claim about the obsolescence of the Sabbath (as the above story does with regard to purity codes), Jesus is shown to be frequently in controversy with other Jews concerning what sanctifies and what profanes the Sabbath. Luke, for example, preserves three such incidents (6:6–11; 13:10–17; 14:1–6). The real model of being in line with God's rhythm of life is not to rigidly separate work and rest (which distinguishes the Jew from the remainder of the world as well), but always to be engaged in mercy and acts of compassion, certainly never to withhold mercy and compassion for the sake of any rigid observance of a commandment. That automatically puts one out of order with regard to God. This comes out especially in Luke 13:10–17, where Jesus' critics address the crowd: "There are six days on which work ought to be done; come on those days and be cured, and not on the sabbath day." Jesus asserts that it is false to think that withholding compassion for the sake of not doing work on the Sabbath (and thus resting with God) is actually a true reflection of what God is doing. God is the merciful and compassionate one, and so mercy and compassion are never out of season, never a violation but always the fulfillment of God's commandment. Those who oppose Jesus' teaching on what truly puts one in line with God's heart are here explicitly "put to shame."

This view of the true keeping of Torah comes to expression again in Luke's "sermon on the plain," not only in the statement of the Golden Rule ("Do to others as you would have them do to you," 6:31) but even more to the point in 6:36: "Be merciful, just as your Father is merciful." Luke shows Jesus thus rewriting or reinterpreting the command in Leviticus 11:44–45 to "be holy, for I am holy" in order to highlight God's mercy as the central characteristic that is to emerge in the children of God. Matthew also underscores this principle as the rule by which Torah is to be applied. Twice Jesus is shown taking the Pharisees to task for missing this interpretative key: "Go and learn what this means, 'I desire mercy, not sacrifice.' For I have come to call not the righteous but sinners" (Mt. 9:13; see also 12:7–8, 11–12). Jesus invokes a passage from the prophet Hosea to prove that the kind of purity that God calls for does not involve shutting oneself away from the presence of sinners. God's purposes of calling the sinner back from death to life would go unfulfilled if such an interpretation of "being holy" were maintained.

Paul speaks with perhaps the most decisive voice in regard to the place of Torah observance in the Christian community. As far as Paul is concerned, the Torah was a temporary measure designed to preserve the distinctiveness of the Jewish people between the promise given to Abraham and the fulfillment of that promise in Jesus, and thence in the community of Jews and Gentiles called together in his name. In Pauline Christianity, the focus of responding to God shifts entirely away from the observance of commandments (although these remain informative guidelines for conduct) toward following the leading of the Holy Spirit, perhaps one of God's most valuable gifts bestowed on the Christian. By walking in line with God's Spirit, the Christian is able to fulfill the just requirement of God's Law without actually relying on observing Torah as the path by which to accomplish this. Romans 8:2–4 is quite to the point here:

> For the law of the Spirit of life in Christ Jesus has set you free from the law of sin and of death. For God has done what the law, weakened by the flesh, could not do: by sending his own Son in the likeness of sinful flesh, and to deal with sin, he condemned sin in the flesh, so that the just requirement of the law might be fulfilled in us, who walk not according to the flesh but according to the Spirit.

Torah did not provide the human being with the resources by which the flesh could be brought in line with God's righteousness and righteous demands, but the Holy Spirit can and does (see also Gal. 5:16–6:10).

"Discipleship" (responding to God's favors and promises) within the Christian community could thus take on a form that was different from the way of life of the Torah-observant Jew. Although the early church maintained the value of Torah (together with the Psalms and Prophets) as a source for learning about God's values, it was now possible to pursue the embodiment of those values by avenues other than becoming Jewish.

"Imitation of God" remained a prominent way in which early Christian leaders guided the recipients of God's favor to respond to God. Such imitation is presented as the way to acknowledge what God has done for the believer and to honor the One who now stands as "Father" over the Christian community. As Christians seek to imitate God's character, they are indeed "justified" in the sense of being brought in line with a rule or standard, namely God's own example and character. Imitation of God now focuses, however, on God's holiness as expressed in God's outreaching love and favor—no longer on holiness as expressed in making distinctions between what is clean and unclean.

Imitation of God begins by practicing forgiveness. This is perhaps the most well-known aspect of responding to God's favors through imitation of God's character (and thus, again, making visible in the world the character of the invisible God). Jesus' parable of the unforgiving servant, who had been forgiven an enormous debt by his master but then refused to release a fellow slave from a relatively minuscule debt, underscores the importance of forgiving others as God forgives us:

> "Then his lord summoned him and said to him, 'You wicked slave! I forgave you all that debt because you pleaded with me. Should you not have had mercy on your fellow slave, as I had mercy on you?' And in anger his lord handed him over to be tortured until he would pay his entire debt. So my heavenly Father will also do to every one of you, if you do not forgive your brother or sister from your heart." (Mt. 18:32–35)

This injunction appears again in the epistolary literature, in the middle of the portrayal of the life of discipleship in Ephesians 4:32–5:1: "Be kind to one another, tenderhearted, forgiving one another, as God in Christ has forgiven you. Therefore be imitators of God, as beloved children" (see also Col. 3:13: "Forgive each other; just as the Lord has forgiven you, so you also must forgive."). These texts direct the recipients of God's grant of pardon to respond to that gift by mirroring it in their own horizontal relationships. The parable told by Jesus particularly underscores the "master's" interest in seeing this response, as well as posing the startling consequences of failing to imitate the master–one's old debts are reinstated!

Jesus also directs his hearers (and thus the early church that preserved these words) to imitate God's generosity. Forgiveness is indeed already an aspect of this generosity, but Jesus extends it to positive acts of kindness and favor:

> "But I say to you, Love your enemies and pray for those who persecute you, so that you may be children of your Father in heaven; for he makes his sun rise on the evil and on the good, and sends rain on the righteous and on the unrighteous. For if you love those who love you, what reward do you have? Do not even the tax collectors do the same? And if you greet only your brothers and sisters, what more are you doing than others? Do not even the Gentiles do the same? Be perfect, therefore, as your heavenly Father is perfect." (Mt. 5:44–48)

> "But love your enemies, do good, and lend, expecting nothing in return. Your reward will be great, and you will be children of the Most High; for he is kind to the ungrateful and the wicked. Be merciful, just as your Father is merciful." (Lk. 6:35–36)

The basis for Jesus' teaching against retaliation of any kind–not to return hate for hate or injury for injury–is the character of God, who extends favor to all. Just as God sends the blessings of rain and sun on the whole world, so God's children are to participate in God's work of bringing blessing, extending favor and mercy as God extends them. This is not a call to be pushovers or doormats, but a call to actively respond to the ignorant, the malicious, and the hurtful with the favor and love of God, which can transform an enemy into a friend, the arrogant into the penitent.

Jesus says that his followers should not respond to the offender according to the offense, because that would mean allowing the evil that motivated the offender to act to shape the disciple's actions as well. The model for the disciple's action is God, who does not respond to people as they deserve, but as God desires in God's love and mercy, calling them to repentance and to wholeness. Followers of Jesus must reflect this aspect of God's character in order to "do the will of the Father." Because God is "perfect" or "whole," God does not depend on others to treat God kindly in order to treat them kindly in return. Disciples of Jesus are called to find their wholeness in God, so that they, too, do not rely on another person to be courteous, understanding, or even just in order for them to seek and to serve God's purposes for that other.

The New Testament authors especially emphasize the showing of love within the Christian community as an essential aspect of imitating God:

> Beloved, let us love one another, because love is from God; everyone who loves is born of God and knows God...In this is love, not that we loved God but that he loved us and sent his Son to be the atoning sacrifice for our sins. Beloved, since God loved us so much, we also ought to love one another. (1 Jn. 4:7, 10–11)

Once again, the disciple is directed to respond to God's gifts (here, the gift of love manifested in the sending of Jesus) by imitating the Giver in dealing with other human beings. One "repays the favor," in effect, by giving what one has received from God to others (whether that be forgiveness, self-sacrificing love, help in time of trouble, or daily sustenance). John goes so far as to declare that those who fail to imitate God on this point of showing love have not, in fact, encountered the loving God: "Whoever does not love does not know God, for God is love" (1 Jn. 4:8).

The motif of imitation of God also upholds the disciples' commitment to pursue a life of righteous acts and to avoid that which has been identified as "sin" in the oracles of God (the Old Testament) and the teaching of Jesus.

> God is light and in him there is no darkness at all. If we say that we have fellowship with him while we are walking in darkness, we lie and do not do what is true; but if we walk in the light as he himself is in the light, we have fellowship with one another, and the blood of Jesus his Son cleanses us from all sin. (1 Jn. 1:5–7).

> If you know that he is righteous, you may be sure that everyone who does right has been born of him... Beloved, we are God's children now; what we will be has not yet been revealed. What we do know is this: when he is revealed, we will be like him, for we will see him as he is. And all who have this hope in him purify themselves, just as he is pure. (1 Jn. 2:29, 3:2–3)

The character of God, "light" and "purity" as opposed to "darkness" and "sin" must be reflected in God's children (1 Jn. 2:9–11; 3:4–10). As in Matthew 5:44–48, the principle of "like parent, like child" appears as the underlying logic of this response to God. ; Having received the gift of being born into God's family, the disciples are to grow into the likeness of their new Parent in every respect.

Whereas John leaves this discussion rather general, the author of 1 Peter urges his congregations to imitate God specifically in order to help them resist the temptation to return to their former way of life (something toward which their neighbors have been vigorously pressing them):

> Like obedient children, do not be conformed to the desires that you formerly had in ignorance. Instead, as he who called you is holy, be holy yourselves in all your conduct; for it is written, "You shall be holy, for I am holy." If you invoke as Father the one who judges all people impartially according to their deeds, live in reverent fear during the time of your exile. (1 Pet 1:14–17)

The Levitical injunction to be holy as God is holy—the birthplace of the theme of imitation of God as the proper response to the God who called together this particular community—is now brought directly into New Testament discourse as the call to separate oneself from one's pre-conversion lifestyle and conform to the new way of life espoused within the Christian group (see 1 Pet. 2:1–3; 4:3–5). This includes continued abstinence from idolatry, from prohibited expressions of sexuality, and from participation in the social gatherings of non-Christian Gentile neighbors. Mirroring God's holiness has thus recaptured the social dimension it had for ancient Israel, namely, maintaining the boundaries between the group and the outside world. Once again, the principle of "like parent, like child" is subtly introduced into the call to imitation: The believers are likened to "obedient children" (1:14) of the God they call "Father" (1:17).

A similar use of the imitation of God motif appears in Ephesians and Colossians (two letters attributed to Paul that show clear signs of literary dependence, one on the other). The ethics of Colossians stems from the disciples' being clothed "with the new self, which is being renewed in knowledge according to the image of its creator" (3:10). Because the disciple has put on a new identity, one that is shaped by the God who gave new life to him or her, that disciple is called to put away all that belonged to the old self (reflecting the sin and strife of the world, as it were) and seek to conform fully to the holy, loving, compassionate God. Ephesians 4:24 uses the same image, again to drive a wedge between the believers and the characteristics that marked and marred their pre-Christian lives (Eph. 4:17–19, 22) and to impel the believers on to the way of life that reflects God's character (Eph. 4:23–24).

In sum, then, while the early Christians moved away from strict Torah observance as the way in which they might make an appropriate response to the God who lavished such favor on them, they retained the essential dynamic of the Jewish response, namely, the imitation of God's holiness. That holiness was reconfigured in a way that emphasized God's generosity, forgiveness, love, and commitment to righteousness, and the recipients of God's favors were called to manifest God's virtue to the world around them in all their relationships.

"Bearing the Death of Christ in Our Mortal Bodies"

In addition to their distinctive vision of what it meant to imitate God's holiness as God's people, early Christians held a second lens up to the light of God's holiness in the person of Jesus. Discipleship meant reflecting the character of God, to be sure, but that character was believed to have been revealed with ultimate clarity in the character of Jesus, in whom "the fullness of God was pleased to dwell" (Col. 1:19), whose way was ultimately vindicated by God as the righteous way *par excellence.*

Paul repeatedly turns to the pattern of Jesus as the goal of discipleship, the end point of the pursuit of righteousness:

> Those whom God foreknew God also predestined to be conformed to the image of God's Son, in order that he might be the firstborn within a large family. (Rom. 8:29)
>
> All of us, with unveiled faces, seeing the glory of the Lord as though reflected in a mirror, are being transformed into the same image from one degree of glory to another. (2 Cor. 3:18)
>
> My little children, for whom I am again in the pain of childbirth until Christ is formed in you. (Gal. 4:19)

Transformation into the likeness of Jesus is repeatedly held up within the Pauline epistles as that which the journey of discipleship is to accomplish. Other New Testament voices also speak of the "imitating" of Jesus as the watchword of the Christian's response to God's call. John, for example, regards this as the natural expectation of the follower of Jesus: "By this we may be sure that we are in him: whoever says, 'I abide in him,' ought to walk just as he walked" (1 Jn. 2:5–6).

The focal point of this second lens is the death of Jesus. Joining oneself to the death of Jesus—assimilation to and reflection of the ultimate obedience of the Righteous One—was seen to be the path to righteousness and to the grant of honor that God would bestow on all who obeyed him: "I want to know Christ and the power of his resurrection and the sharing of his sufferings *by becoming like him in his death*, if somehow I may attain the resurrection from the dead" (Phil. 3:10–11; emphasis mine).

Mark prominently focuses in his gospel on the voluntary, obedient death of Jesus as the interpretative key to Christian discipleship. The middle section of Mark (8:22–10:52) shows signs of careful literary structuring. The whole section is marked off by two narratives about the healing of blind men (8:22–26; 10:46–52). Within the section, three predictions by Jesus of his impending suffering, death, and resurrection (8:31–33; 9:30–32; 10:32–34) are closely followed by three teachings about the nature of Christian discipleship (8:34–9:1; 9:33–37; 10:35–45). There is little doubt that Mark's structure thus reinforces the fundamental conviction that following Jesus as a disciple means incarnating the attitude and obedience seen in the Messiah.

Moreover, the first teaching on discipleship makes this connection explicit: "'If any want to become my followers, let them deny themselves and take up their cross and follow me. For those who want to save their life will lose it, and those who lose their life for my sake, and for the sake of the gospel, will save it'" (Mk. 8:34–35). The meaning of "denying oneself" and "taking up one's cross" remains murky at this first announcement. Mark indeed presents the disciples as being confused concerning the nature of the life to which they are called, failing to grasp the practical implications of Jesus' summons. After Jesus' second announcement of his coming execution and God's vindication, the disciples display their misunderstanding by arguing with one another over who will be Jesus' "number one" within the group. Jesus responds by telling them that their competitions for precedence over one another are the reverse of what God values in a person, which is the willingness to put his or her own interests last and serve the interests of the other (Mk. 9:35). This would be a difficult word in an honor culture such as the first-century Greco-Roman world, where competition for honor and recognition was the expected, normal, even virtuous dynamic between people who were not related to each other. Nevertheless, Jesus insists that such is not the path to honor before God.

After a third announcement of the degradation, death, and vindication that await him, Jesus finds John and James trying to jockey for a position of honor within the kingdom (Mk. 10:35–40). The anger of the other disciples does not show their correct grasp of God's way, but instead their resentment that John and James almost won the competition. Here Jesus brings together once more the connection between his own example and the life of discipleship: "Whoever wishes to become great among you must be your servant, and whoever wishes to be first among you must be slave of all. For the Son of Man came not to be served but to serve, and to give his life a ransom for many" (Mk. 10:43–45). Jesus' life of service for others, which was about to be demonstrated once more as he halted his own procession into Jerusalem to care for a blind beggar (10:46–52) and which would be consummated as he willingly endured mocking, abuse, and crucifixion in obedience to God's purposes and in service to the human race, had to be replicated in his disciples. It would never do to have the master seek to serve but the followers seek to rule (see Jn. 13:12–17)! Thus, Mark has shown through this central narrative that following the crucified Messiah—taking up the cross and denying self—means setting aside one's own desires for honor and recognition, one's own interests and preferences, and serving others.

This is an emphasis shared by all four evangelists, as shown by the fact that Matthew and Luke have retained those narratives from Mark's gospel. John, however, introduces the emphasis in a rather different setting, namely, on the night before Jesus was handed over to suffering and death. During dinner, Jesus takes on the role of a domestic servant: Taking off his robe, he wraps a towel around himself and begins to wash the feet of each disciple. After this moment—the discomfort of which is evidenced by Peter's outbursts—Jesus explains the lesson to the disciples:

> "Do you know what I have done to you? You call me Teacher and Lord—and you are right, for that is what I am. So if I, your Lord and Teacher, have washed your feet, you also ought to wash one another's feet. For I have set you an example, that you also should do as I have done to you. Very truly, I tell you, servants are not greater than their master, nor are messengers greater than the one who sent them. If you know these things, you are blessed if you do them." (Jn. 13:12–17)

The way of discipleship is not to be the path to self-fulfillment or self-promotion. Jesus' example shows it to be the path of self-denial and service to others. This episode quite clearly emphasizes the aspect of setting aside any privileges or claims one might have by virtue of one's dignity, and choosing instead to take on the role of a servant to others. The aspect of choice is significant here—Jesus is not offering his example to make the role of oppressors easier by urging humble compliance and acceptance of subordination on the part of the subjected. Following Jesus' example, the example of the master who chooses to serve, does entail the transvaluation of worldly hierarchies in favor of seeing all as worthy recipients of service, respect, and investment rather than protecting oneself from performing certain acts of service considered "beneath" oneself.

When we find the same aspect of discipleship echoed in Paul's writings, we know that we have indeed come across something that was central to the Christian response to God in the New Testament. Paul most clearly articulates this in his application of the example or pattern of Christ in Philippians 2:1–11. This is perhaps one of the more celebrated passages in Paul's letters because it contains the "Christ hymn" that has become the basis for many Christian confessions and hymns:

> Though he was in the form of God, [Jesus] did not regard equality with God as something to be exploited, but emptied himself, taking the form of a slave, being born in human likeness. And being found in human form, he humbled himself and became obedient to the point of death—even death on a cross. Therefore God also highly exalted him and gave him the name that is above every name, so that at the name of Jesus every knee should bend, in heaven and on earth and under the earth, and every tongue should confess that Jesus Christ is Lord, to the glory of God the Father. (Phil. 2:6–11)

The story of the One whom Christians call "Lord" is the story of one who does not cling to the rights and privileges of his status, who does not insist on recognition of his own precedence. Instead, it is the story of one who chooses (again, voluntariness is essential) to take on the role of a servant and slave, who chooses obedience to God even if it means the loss of all recognition and honor in the eyes of the world (an obvious component of crucifixion).

Paul understands that the pattern of Jesus must be replicated in the lives of his followers, particularly in their life together as congregations. Writing to his friends in Philippi—a church that had been marvelously supportive of Paul and his ministry—he brings the pattern of Jesus to bear on the lack of unity and cooperation that has broken out within the church there. Two leaders of the local congregation have become rivals rather than partners (see Phil. 4:2–3), and this conflict either has already spread, or at least has the potential to spread, throughout the congregation and undermine the strength of the Christian community there (see the frequent appeals for unity and harmony: Phil. 1:27; 2:1–2, 14–15). Paul points to the example of Jesus leading in an entirely different direction: "Do nothing from selfish ambition or conceit, but in humility regard others as better than yourselves. Let each of you look not to your own interests, but to the interests of others. Let the same mind be in you that was in Christ Jesus" (Phil. 2:3–5). The Christ hymn quoted above now follows. Where such a mind is enfleshed among Jesus' followers, there can be no rivalry, no sense of injured merit, no insistence on having one's own way, no calculation of what will be personally advantageous. In short, there will not be any of the attitudes or behaviors that sacrifice the harmony and strength of the community for the private interests or agendas of one or a few. Rather than consider one's own claims to precedence in the community, or one's own right to direct what the community should do, one considers the honor of sisters and brothers in the faith and how best to serve God's purposes for them.

Jesus' death was understood as the measure of his love for humankind, a love that had been acknowledged among the believers. It was this measure of love that was to be adopted by Christians for one another:

> Live in love, as Christ loved us and gave himself up for us, a fragrant offering and sacrifice to God. (Eph. 5:2)
>
> We know love by this, that he laid down his life for us—and we ought to lay down our lives for one another. How does God's love abide in anyone who has the world's goods and sees a brother or sister in need and yet refuses help? Little children, let us love, not in word or speech, but in truth and action. (1 Jn. 3:16–18)

As Jesus showed self-giving, sacrificial love to the believers, so the believers were to show love toward one another as part of their grateful response to Jesus. John's writings are particularly noteworthy for the practical way in which John envisions such love being manifested. "Laying down one's life" for the sister or brother means laying out one's resources, energies, and personal investment for another. It means regarding what one has as that which is given to relieve the needs or promote the good of another.

Joining oneself to Jesus in his death thus powerfully serves to reinforce an ethos of service, love, and care for the sister or brother and, indeed, for all. In Pauline texts, another direction in which replicating the pattern of Jesus' death moves is also important for the formation of "discipleship" in the New Testament. In his letter to the Christians in Galatia, Paul writes that "those who belong to Christ Jesus have crucified the flesh with its passions and desires" (Gal. 5:24). Identification with the crucified Messiah results here in the "crucifixion" (the "putting to death") of the passions and yearnings of the "flesh." By "flesh," Paul means not our physical bodies but the sum total of those aspects of a person's being that lead a person away from what God approves and values in a person. "Flesh" thus includes selfish ambition, self-gratification, the objectification of other people that permits everything from anger and envy to sexual license (see Gal. 5:16–21). Jesus' death in the flesh must be reflected, then, in the disciple's death to the "flesh" and to the lifestyle that "flesh" nurtures. Paul invites his readers to make his mode of existence their own: "I have been crucified with Christ; and it is no longer I who live, but it is Christ who lives in me. And the life I now live in the flesh I live by faith in the Son of God, who loved me and gave himself for me" (Gal. 2:19–20).

This concept is more fully explored in Paul's later letter to the Christians in Rome:

> How can we who died to sin go on living in it?...We know that our old self was crucified with him so that the body of sin might be destroyed, and we might no longer be enslaved to sin...So you also must consider yourselves dead to sin and alive to God in Christ Jesus. Therefore, do not let sin exercise dominion in your mortal bodies, to make you obey their passions. No longer present your members to sin as instruments of wickedness, but present yourselves to God as those who have been brought from death to life, and present your members to God as instruments of righteousness. (Rom. 6:2, 6, 11–13)

The replication in the disciple's life of Jesus' death and resurrection appears in his or her dying to the sinful inclinations and walking in line with a new set of inclinations implanted by God's spirit. The believers who have joined themselves to Jesus in his death will no longer do the work or will of sin in the world, any more than a corpse will hang drywall or paint a house. Being "dead to sin" is simultaneously accompanied, however, by a coming to life—a resurrection, as it were—of the life of holiness and justice that pleases God and serves God's interests in the world. The believer is encouraged to commit himself or herself to enfleshing the death and resurrection of Jesus in this way through the incentive of the hope of the final resurrection from the dead: "If we have been united with him in a death like his, we will certainly be united with him in a resurrection like his" (Rom. 6:5).

The example of Jesus—the Messiah devalued, degraded, and brutalized by society but approved, exalted, and vindicated by God—also serves to orient disciples toward the hostility and censure they experience from the non-Christian world as a result of their confession. Jesus' own example becomes proof that the dominant culture cannot make a reliable evaluation of a person's worth, and therefore that honor or dishonor in the eyes of the non-Christian are matters of indifference. That the world failed to honor him who sat at God's right hand in the place of highest honor, and instead subjected him to the worst disgrace and abuse it could devise, shows, in the end, the world's ignorance of what is honorable and what is shameful. When the disciples of this Messiah, then, encounter the same experiences of censure and hostility, they should be armed with the understanding that the world's attempts to shame them have no true bearing on their honor (and the nobility of their life choices) in God's sight.

The evangelists use the pattern of Jesus to insulate the disciples from outside pressures to conform to what the dominant culture deems respectable. Matthew, for example, preserves this saying of Jesus:

> "A disciple is not above the teacher, nor a slave above the master; it is enough for the disciple to be like the teacher, and the slave like the master. If they have called

> the master of the house Beelzebul, how much more will they malign those of his household!" (Mt. 10:24–25)

Similarly, in one of those rare instances where he shares a particular Jesus saying with the synoptic gospels, John writes,

> "Remember the word that I said to you, 'Servants are not greater than their master.' If they persecuted me, they will persecute you; if they kept my word, they will keep yours also. But they will do all these things to you on account of my name, because they do not know him who sent me." (Jn. 15:20–21)
>
> "They will put you out of the synagogues. Indeed, an hour is coming when those who kill you will think that by doing so they are offering worship to God. And they will do this because they have not known the Father or me. But I have said these things to you so that when their hour comes you may remember that I told you about them." (Jn. 16:2–4)

Matthew and John give the message, first, that enduring censure and persecution from nondisciples is only fitting, given what befalls the "master" himself. It would be unjust, in a sense, for the disciples to seek to have an easier time of life than their master had. Second, these writers give their audiences a sense that such a negative response from their non-Christian neighbors is to be expected. They should not be caught off guard by this response or question the correctness of their decision to follow this Jesus. Rather, they now have an interpretive context for making sense of their experiences of rejection—the paradigm of Jesus himself.

The author of 1 Peter makes extensive use of the example of Jesus in his call to endure hostility and deprivation for the sake of one's commitment to Jesus and the way of life approved by God (which would include the avoidance of all forms of idolatry, or what non-Christian Gentiles would call "piety" and "duty"). Addressing slaves whose Christian commitment might lead them to nonparticipation in the household's domestic religion, and thus to conflict with the head of the household, Peter writes,

> If you endure when you are beaten for doing wrong, what credit is that? But if you endure when you do right and suffer for it, you have God's approval. For to this you have been called, because Christ also suffered for you, leaving you an example, so that you should follow in his steps. "He committed no sin, and no deceit was found in his mouth." When he was abused, he did not return abuse; when he suffered, he did not threaten; but he entrusted himself to the one who judges justly. (1 Pet. 2:20–23)

Jesus' own response to the hostility, cajoling, and challenges of other Jewish leaders throughout his life is remembered here as part of Jesus' example; the main emphasis is, of course, on his trial and death. These are all specifically invoked in order to provide an example for the slaves in the household who might be suffering at the hands of their masters because of their new commitment to Jesus as Master. Reminding them of Jesus' endurance of all this *on their behalf* at this point in the text cannot be accidental: "He himself bore our sins in his body on the cross, so that, free from sins, we might live for righteousness; by his wounds you have been healed. For you were going astray like sheep, but now you have returned to the shepherd and guardian of your souls" (1 Pet. 2:24–25; see how this topic emerges also in 2 Cor. 5:15 and Gal. 2:19–20). Continued loyalty and obedience to Jesus in the face of human opposition is not urged merely on the basis of following Christ's example but also on the basis of making a fair and honorable return to Jesus for his generosity toward his disciples—the acts of beneficence that initiated the relationship in the first place.

Nor does Peter limit his application of the pattern of Jesus to Christian slaves only. In the remaining parts of the letter, his exhortations to that particularly vulnerable group become his exhortations to all disciples (see also 1 Peter 3:8–9; 4:14–16 for parallels between the exhortations to slaves quoted above and exhortations to the congregations as a whole):

> Since therefore Christ suffered in the flesh, arm yourselves also with the same intention (for whoever has suffered in the flesh has finished with sin), so as to

> live for the rest of your earthly life no longer by human desires but by the will of God...Rejoice insofar as you are sharing Christ's sufferings, so that you may also be glad and shout for joy when his glory is revealed...Let those suffering in accordance with God's will entrust themselves to a faithful Creator, while continuing to do good. (1 Pet. 4:1–2, 13, 19)

When the end of Jesus' story is kept in view, the example of Jesus becomes an especially powerful source of resistance to the outside world's attempts to wear down the believers' allegiance to him. Such a view of the future is subtly woven in here in 1 Peter 4:13 (Peter can afford this subtlety, because he has already developed this hope at some length in 1:3–7; 3:21–22). Christ's resurrection and the promise of the believer's partnership with Christ in that resurrection and eternal honor (provided he or she is willing to be seen as his partner now in a hostile world) are used throughout the New Testament to demonstrate and affirm the advantage of following Jesus' example (see also Col. 3:1–4; 2 Thess. 1:5–12; Heb. 12:1–2; Rev. 2:26–28; 3:21).

While the example of Jesus insulates believers from the opinion outsiders may form of them (and seek to impress on them through various forms of social pressure), it also teaches the ultimate unimportance and unreliability of visible impressions and evaluations based on these impressions within the community of disciples. A crucified Savior made no sense to either Jew or Greek–to whom it was revolting and seemed like madness–but was precisely the way in which God revealed divine wisdom to the world and reconciled the world to God's Self (see 1 Cor. 1:18–25). Looking at Jesus from a worldly point of view, that is, evaluating Jesus according to the standards of strength, beauty, worth, and success as defined by either Greco-Roman or Jewish culture, resulted in a low opinion of this Jesus. In God's sight, however, the picture looked very different. Paul sought to bring this aspect of the gospel home especially for the Christians in Corinth, who seemed content to continue to rate one another and their leaders according to the criteria used by the non-Christian majority. The crucified Christ revealed, however, that appearances in the flesh were no true indication of a person's worth in God's evaluation, that, indeed, God's power was more likely to break through into the world to transform it and to give new life to humanity precisely where human pretensions of perfection and strength did not get in the way (see especially 2 Cor. 4:7–18; 12:1–10).

Another important source of information for how one is to respond faithfully as a disciple are the stories about Jesus' own life and example. Transformation into the likeness of Jesus is informed and facilitated not only by reflection on the values and attitudes shown in his willing acceptance of death on behalf of others in obedience to God but also by reflection on what Jesus did when confronted with a variety of situations. The basic conviction expressed in 1 John 2:6 underscores the importance of stories about Jesus as nurture for a distinctive, Christian ethos: "Whoever says, 'I abide in him,' ought to walk just as he walked." We have already seen in the excerpts from 1 Peter above that Jesus' own example of non-retaliation is normative for the followers of Christ as well. When their own honor is challenged (e.g., by a physical affront), they are not to respond in kind but rather to respond with benevolence. The portrayal of Jesus as one who makes it a central aim to restore the sinners and the lost to a place in God's family and in the community of God leads to frequent exhortations to do the same now within the community of disciples:

> My friends, if anyone is detected in a transgression, you who have received the Spirit should restore such a one in a spirit of gentleness...Bear one another's burdens, and in this way you will fulfill the law of Christ. (Gal. 6:1–2)
>
> My brothers and sisters, if anyone among you wanders from the truth and is brought back by another, you should know that whoever brings back a sinner from wandering will save the sinner's soul from death and will cover a multitude of sins. (Jas. 5:19–20)

The disciple's response to the beneficence of God and of God's Anointed, then, is in large measure shaped by the theme of imitation. This is imitation first of God's own character, beneficence, and outreaching love–a transposition of the ancient Israelite and early Jewish focus on imitating God's holiness as that which observes the distinction between clean and unclean, sacred and profane. This imitation is given sharper focus in the example of Jesus, in the quest to follow the example of his life but even more in the attempt to "bear Jesus' death in one's own mortal body" (see 2 Cor. 4:10) in all the aspects this might include, all in the hope of sharing also in Jesus' life beyond death and in the honor of the Son of God.

Calling Jesus "Lord"

The shape of the disciple's response to God in the New Testament goes beyond instructions based on the imitation or reflection of the One God and God's Messiah, although this has proven to be a rather consistent and pervasive aspect of discipleship. From imitation of Christ, that is, obedience to Christ's example, one could move to the necessity of obedience to Christ's words. Both Matthew and Luke preserve a saying that evidences Jesus' expectation in this regard: "Why do you call me 'Lord, Lord,' and do not do what I tell you?" (Lk. 6:46; see Mt. 7:21–23). The confession that "Jesus is Lord" (1 Cor. 12:3) is thus meaningless apart from the commitment to obey this one whom the disciple names his or her "lord," that is, "master" or "ruler." The recollection of Jesus' words, then, becomes an important guidepost for the life of the disciple, who leaves self-determination aside and commits to living as Jesus commanded.

Although a full survey of these words would be out of place here, one may take as but one example Jesus' sayings about wealth and discipleship and their application in the early church. Luke is especially important for reflections on how the believer is to relate to and use possessions. As early as John the Baptist's preaching, one finds Luke already giving clear direction concerning how one is to live out repentance from sin and rededication to God: "And the crowds asked him, 'What then should we do?' In reply he said to them, 'Whoever has two coats must share with anyone who has none; and whoever has food must do likewise'" (Lk. 3:10–11). This sounds a theme that will resonate throughout the gospel of Luke, who will even bring sayings and parables that in Mark or Matthew speak to some other issue into the orbit of commending care for the poor and the investing of one's resources in relief of the needy. For example, when a Pharisee takes exception to Jesus' disregard for ritual washings before meals, Jesus replies, "'Now you Pharisees clean the outside of the cup and of the dish, but inside you are full of greed and wickedness. You fools! Did not the one who made the outside make the inside also? So give for alms those things that are within; and see, everything will be clean for you'" (11:39–41). Unlike the parallels in Mark and Matthew, the goal here is not a broad redefinition of purity (or setting aside of dietary laws). Rather, uncleanness is very specifically redefined as "greed and wickedness," and purity is the result specifically of giving aid to the poor.

Luke alone preserves Jesus' parable of the foolish rich man. In response to being summoned by a bystander to become arbiter in an inheritance dispute, Jesus points to the folly of storing up wealth as the world counts it but being found poor toward God on the day when the naked soul is stripped of life and possessions and stands before God (12:13–21). How does one become rich toward God? Matthew counsels laying up treasures in heaven (6:19–21), but Luke adds a clear and specific direction for how one can do so: "*Sell your possessions, and give alms.* Make purses for yourselves that do not wear out, an unfailing treasure in heaven, where no thief comes near and no moth destroys. For where your treasure is, there your heart will be also" (12:33–34).

This startling injunction to "sell your possessions and give alms" in 12:33 continues to be reinforced. First, Luke places as the conclusion to his discussion of counting the cost of discipleship the saying "So therefore, none of you can become my disciple if you do not give up all your possessions" (14:33). Discipleship means laying no further claim to one's possessions as one's own, but putting them entirely into the hands of God's discretionary fund. Later, Luke preserves the challenge to the rich young man: "Sell all that you own and distribute the money to the poor, and you will have treasure in heaven; then come, follow me" (18:22). Because the reader has already heard this same challenge issued to all twice before, he or she will not suppose that Jesus directs it only at this particular rich person, but rather that he directs it to all who become part of the community of faith. Finally, one encounters the positive counterpart to this rich man in 19:2–10, namely Zacchaeus. Zacchaeus, a model convert, does not sell *all* his possessions, but he does sell half of them and give the proceeds as alms for the poor. The pattern of Zacchaeus is perhaps remembered as a model of how Jesus' sayings about possessions and laying up treasures in heaven may be applied in everyday life. Jesus calls us to cut away excesses in order to provide for others' necessities, to "live simply so that others may simply live." In a way, Zacchaeus poses a much more potent challenge to the reader than the rich young man does. While few, if any, could sell *all* their possessions and give to the poor, it would be possible, though difficult, for many to give away much of their possessions and still provide for their necessities, making it all the more real a challenge.

Throughout the New Testament, one finds Christian communities falling in line with, or being called to fall in line with, Jesus' commands concerning possessions. The idealized portrait of the earliest Christian community in Jerusalem shows a clear commitment to this ethic of sharing possessions:

> The whole group of those who believed were of one heart and soul, and no one claimed private ownership of any possessions, but everything they owned was held in common...There was not a needy person among them, for as many as owned lands or houses sold them and brought the proceeds of what was sold...and it was distributed to each as any had need. (Acts 4:32, 34–35)

The Deuteronomic ideal for the community of God was thus fulfilled in the early church (see Deut. 15:4–5). Keeping and hoarding wealth was denounced as inimical to the Christian ethos. The possessions one stockpiles and the riches one keeps to oneself become physical "evidence" for the prosecution on the day of judgment (Jas. 5:1–6), a proof that one has not walked in love for neighbor. Instead, disciples are called to imitate Jesus' love by using their own possessions as the means by which to relieve the needs of the family of God (1 Jn. 3:16–18). The author of 1 Timothy shows the ongoing importance of Jesus' commands concerning wealth a full generation after the birth of the church: "As for those who in the present age are rich...they are to do good, to be rich in good works, generous, and ready to share, thus storing up for themselves the treasure of a good foundation for the future, so that they may take hold of the life that really is life" (1 Tim. 6:17–19). The echo of Jesus' saying here is unmistakable, as well as the expectation that his words—on every subject—will be obeyed by those who call him "Lord."

In summary, then, the disciple's response to the favor of God, specifically as this was manifested in the death of Jesus, must be the return of life for life. Since Jesus died on behalf of the disciples, they are obliged now to live for Jesus, even to seek to permit Jesus to live through them (2 Cor. 5:15; Gal. 2:19–20). Here, the imitation motif richly informs what such a life would look like. The disciples are called on to show unflinching loyalty to Jesus and the One God in the midst of an idolatrous culture (1 Cor. 10:14–22; Rev. 13:1–14:13), a society that invokes many gods and exerts pressure on the (Gentile-born) disciples to continue to do the same. As recipients of great gifts, they are challenged to bear witness to those gifts and to the goodness of the Giver (1 Pet. 2:9–10), even in a situation in which such testimony will alienate them from natural kin and neighbors (Mt. 10:26–33). Finally, the disciple understands that, by calling Jesus "Lord," he or she has placed himself or herself in the service of this Lord, who directs the disciple ever to serve God's household and others toward whom God directs his or her acts of love and kindness (Heb. 6:9–12; 13:16). Just as God's favor is a past, present, and future reality, the disciple responds not only out of gratitude for what has been given but also in hope for the gift that will come at the appearing of Jesus (1 Pet. 1:13). He or she perseveres in the way of life to which God has called the believer both in response to what God has already done and in trust with regard to God's promises concerning the end of that way of life (Heb. 10:26–39).

CHAPTER 3

Church

The People of God

The New Testament authors do not understand Christianity to be the personal religion of individuals, but the way of life espoused, nurtured, and supported within a community of believers. The early church strongly emphasized the social dimension of Christian culture. This community–the group within which each individual finds his or her identity and place of belonging–is characterized by its connections to a particular heritage and its lively awareness of the moving of God in its midst. It is sustained by the intentional promotion of a distinctive interpersonal ethos. The believer's indebtedness to God and Jesus, and specifically his or her adoption into the family of God, lays on the believer an obligation to God's household, to serve the members of God's family as God has directed. This chapter will explore three main questions concerning New Testament community: What identity and place in God's plan do the New Testament texts ascribe to this community? What shape do these texts seek to give to relationships within the community and to the community's relationship with the outside world? What happened as the community came together?

The Church's Identity—Who Is the Heir of God's Promises?

Christian communities developed their understanding of identity in large measure through categories drawn from the traditions that they inherited from Israel. The early church looked to the same scriptures that the Jewish people looked to, and so it was natural that these same scriptures should speak to them concerning their place in God's plan and should supply them with their sense of who they were as a people. Just as the early Christians understood Jesus to be the fulfillment of the hope and the promises articulated in those scriptures (see chapter 1), they also understood their new community, which had accepted and gathered around this Jesus, as the heir to those hopes and those promises. The pattern for this is clearly articulated in Acts 3:19–24:

> Repent therefore, and turn to God so that your sins may be wiped out, so that times of refreshing may come from the presence of the Lord, and that he may send the Messiah appointed for you, that is, Jesus, who must remain in heaven until the time of universal restoration that God announced long ago through his holy prophets. Moses said, "The Lord your God will raise up for you from your own people a prophet like me. You must listen to whatever he tells you. And it will be that everyone who does not listen to that prophet will be utterly rooted out of the people." And all the prophets, as many as have spoken, from Samuel and those after him, also predicted these days.

This application of Deuteronomy 18:15, 18–19 to the experience of the early church accomplishes two important interpretative moves. First, and most obviously, it affirms the connection between Jesus and the content of the Hebrew Scriptures: "God announced long ago through his holy prophets" the passion, death, exaltation, and return of Jesus; Jesus is identified as the prophet whom Moses foretold would arise in his place; "all the prophets" are said to have predicted the things that the early church has heard about and experienced in Jesus.

The Christ-centered interpretation of the scriptures has been covered already (at least in an introductory manner) in chapter 1.

The second interpretative move provides what is critical for the current chapter, namely the redefinition of who constitutes the "people of God"—a redefinition made by God through the great lawgiver himself. The essential criterion for belonging to the people of God is acceptance of this "prophet like Moses," who has already been identified by the speaker in Acts 3 as Jesus. Those who do not respond positively to this Jesus find themselves cut off from the people and thus no longer part of Israel. The importance of anchoring such a claim in an authoritative oracle of God (such as Deut. 18:18–19) cannot be overstated. It is a way of bringing out from the ancient tradition itself a clear sign and token that the new community of disciples stands in continuity with that tradition, a claim thus made not from "outside" the tradition but from "inside."

Within the context of the earliest churches, this "people of God" was likely to have been considered a faithful remnant *within* Israel, much as the Qumran community (the discovery of whose library, commonly referred to as the "Dead Sea Scrolls," has made a tremendous impact on biblical studies in the past five decades) considered itself to be the true keepers of God's covenant *within* a largely apostate Israel. That is to say, only Jews who responded to Jesus would be considered part of this people of God. As the church grew and the question of the place of Gentiles in the community was pressed, however, it would no longer be assumed that being a part of ethnic Israel was a prerequisite to being a part of God's faithful remnant gathered around this Jesus. Instead, responding to Jesus would become the *only* criterion for being part of the people of God.

As we explore the ways in which New Testament authors give shape to Christian identity as the people of God, we find two basic dynamics at work. On the one hand, these authors explain the continuity between the church and the historic people of God whose record is contained in the Hebrew Scriptures. On the other hand, these authors also emphasize that the Christian community is in fact *the* successor to that historic people of God, specifically making this claim over against non-Christian Jews. The first aspect serves an identity-defining goal, while the second serves to support that identity in the face of high tension between church and synagogue, maintaining Christian identity by defining it over against a particularly close "outsider" group.

Paul and the author of Acts especially emphasize the continuity between the church and the ancient people of God. The story of Acts develops as a narrative amplification of the prophecy of Amos explicitly quoted by James in the center and at the essential turning point of that story:

> This agrees with the words of the prophets, as it is written, "After this I will return, and I will rebuild the dwelling of David, which has fallen; from its ruins I will rebuild it, and I will set it up, so that all other peoples may seek the Lord–even all the Gentiles over whom my name has been called. Thus says the Lord, who has been making these things known from long ago." (Acts 15: 15–18)

The first nine chapters of Acts describe the building up of the church in Judea, Galilee, and Samaria (9:31) and thus understand the Jewish Christian churches there to be the rebuilt house of David. Following this phase, James asserts, it is to be expected that all the nations will seek the Lord, which is precisely what one finds from Acts 10 (which tells of the conversion of the Roman centurion, Cornelius, and his household) onward. The growth of the Jesus movement within Palestine and the subsequent mission to the Gentile world are thus presented as the working out of "things known from long ago" within the Jewish tradition, hence a movement in essential continuity with that tradition.

Paul also regards the Christian movement as the natural (indeed, divinely appointed) outworking of his ancestral tradition. An important resource for him in this regard is the Abraham tradition. Abraham, after all, received a promise from God that he would become the father of many nations. The fact that Abraham was accounted righteous in God's sight prior to his circumcision is taken by Paul as a sign that he was to be "the ancestor of all who believe without being circumcised and who thus have righteousness reckoned to them, and likewise the ancestor of the circumcised who are not only circumcised but who also follow the example of the faith that our ancestor Abraham had before he was circumcised" (Rom. 4:11–12). Paul draws a line here around the Christian community—those Gentiles who have trusted God's promises in Jesus without being circumcised together with those Jews who, being circumcised, also trust those promises—as the body of those who are Abraham's descendants. Descent from Abraham is established here no longer on the basis of physical descent (i.e., being born a Jew) or acceptance of circumcision, but on the basis of imitating Abraham's trust in God's power to bring life to the dead.

Paul makes an even more radical claim in his letter to the churches in Galatia. In that situation, Paul seeks to counter claims that have been made by a rival mission that circumcision is the only way by which Gentile Christians can join themselves to the people of God and enjoy the privilege of being included among Abraham's descendants and heirs. Paul argues that, to the contrary, God's promises were not given to the ethnic Jewish people: "The promises were made to Abraham and to his offspring; it does not say, 'And to offsprings,' as of many; but it says, 'And to your offspring,' that is, to one person, who is Christ" (Gal. 3:16). We might balk at the interpretation based on a technicality (an ambiguous one at that, since "offspring" can be either collective or singular), but Paul is nevertheless able to argue from the literal sense of an authoritative text that God's promise is granted to Abraham and to Jesus alone. Inclusion among the heirs of Abraham and of the promise, therefore, can only come through joining oneself to this Jesus: "In Christ Jesus you are all children of God through faith. As many of you as were baptized into Christ have clothed yourselves with Christ... And if you belong to Christ, then you are Abraham's offspring, heirs according to the promise" (Gal. 3:26–27, 29). In a manner very similar to what we encountered in Acts 3 above, Paul claims that Jesus' followers are the ones who stand in clear continuity with the Hebrew Scriptural tradition, and that joining oneself to Jesus is the means by which one joins oneself to the historic people of God.

In Romans 9–11, Paul offers a particularly involved and, indeed, convoluted explanation of God's faithfulness to God's promises to Israel as these are being worked out in the early church. Although Paul's purposes go beyond demonstrating the continuity of the church with historic Israel (focusing chiefly on exploring the mystery of the Jewish people's widespread rejection of the message about Jesus), he still offers important contributions to this theme. First, he offers a reminder that belonging to Israel is not a matter of one's physical lineage. Just as Abraham had numerous sons, but his descendants were only counted through Isaac and Jacob, "not all Israelites truly belong to Israel" (Rom. 9:6). He taps here into the Old Testament theme of the "remnant," the conviction that within ethnic Israel, the majority of whom had strayed from God's ways, God would preserve a minority for himself (see Rom. 9:27–29). As the argument develops, Paul points to the small number of Jews who have responded positively to Jesus' call (offering himself as "Exhibit A") as the remnant that God has reserved from Israel, comparable to the seven thousand Israelites who, in Elijah's time, had not defiled themselves with Baal worship (see Rom. 11:1–6).

This remnant provides the nucleus of the new group of Jews and Gentiles (see also Rev. 7:4–17 for another depiction of the emergence of a remnant from Israel at the core of a multinational people for God), whose inclusion into the people of Israel is, Paul asserts, envisioned from within Israel's prophetic tradition. The assembly of believers, "called not from the Jews only but also from the Gentiles" (Rom. 9:24), is the outworking of Hosea 2:23: "Those who were not my people I will call 'my people,' and her who was not beloved I will call 'beloved.' And in the very place where it was said to them, 'You are not my people,' there they shall be called children of the living God" (as quoted in Rom. 9:25–26). In its original context, the oracle speaks of the restoration of the nation of Israel after her exile, but in Paul's hands it becomes a clear sign of God's intention to include the Gentile nations–who also were once not God's people–among God's people (see also 1 Pet. 2:10).

In developing the continuity between church and the historic people of God, Paul and other New Testament authors draw not only on the remnant theme but also on the "universalism" theme in the Old Testament. This theme, running throughout the Psalms and the prophetic literature of the Old Testament, looked ahead to a time when non-Israelites would come to acknowledge the God of Israel as the One and only God, a time that had indeed arrived within the Christian community. The author of Acts portrays this as an essential component of early Christian missionary preaching to a Gentile audience, calling on them to turn away from idol worship to the worship of the One God who made heaven and earth (see Acts 14:15–17 and 17:22–31). This is also a prominent part of Paul's summary of the conversion experience of Gentile Christians: "You turned to God from idols, to serve a living and true God" (1 Thess. 1:9). Again turning to Paul's letter to the Christians in Rome, one finds Paul connecting the experience of the early church with the tradition of Israel:

> The scripture says, "No one who believes in him will be put to shame." For there is no distinction between Jew and Greek; the same Lord is Lord of all and is generous to all who call on him. For, "Everyone who calls on the name of the Lord shall be saved." (Rom. 10:11–13)

Paul incorporates here two texts from the prophets (Isa. 28:16 and Joel 2:32) that make rather universalistic claims concerning the relationship of humanity to God: the Gentile Christians are clearly invited to see themselves included in Paul's "no one" and "everyone" in these texts. Paul is also appealing to God's impartiality, a quality that must necessarily be predicated of God if God's justice (or fairness) is to be affirmed, as Romans 2 develops at some length.

A fourth resource is invoked here, however, as proof that the Gentiles are also to be part of God's people, namely, God's oneness. The conviction that the "same Lord is Lord of all" is derived from the *Shema* itself, the kernel creed of Judaism found in Deuteronomy 6:4 and recited twice daily by pious Jews around the Mediterranean at that time: "Hear, O Israel: The LORD our God, the LORD is One" (Deut. 6:4, NIV). Paul interprets this creed as the final basis for his claim that God makes Jew and Gentile righteous on the same basis, namely, the basis of their trust in God: "Is God the God of Jews only? Is he not the God of Gentiles also? Yes, of Gentiles also, *since God is one;* and he will justify the circumcised on the ground of faith and the uncircumcised through that same faith" (Rom. 3:29–30). The continuity between the Christian community of Jews and Gentiles and the tradition of Israel is thus tied in at its deepest and most basic level. The Christian community is invited to see itself as representing the fruition and fulfillment of God's vision for God's people as announced in the prophetic tradition, namely, as a body in which "all the nations" are being joined in worship of, and obedience to, the One God (see also Rom. 15:7–13 and Eph. 2:11–22; 3:3, 5–6, 14–15).

As the body that stands in continuity with the historic people of God, the community of disciples becomes heir to the titles and descriptions that had been applied to historic Israel. The names and qualities ascribed to Israel by God and God's messengers, by means of which the Israelites' corporate identity was shaped, now provide the raw material for the shaping of the church's identity. At the same time, these titles, coming as they do from Israel's sacred history, continue to remind the Christians of their spiritual heritage, their continuity with that ancient people of God. John, for example, calls the Christians to whom he writes a kingdom of priests (Rev. 1:5–6; 5:9–10), drawing on God's description of the Hebrew people in Exodus 19:6 as a royal priesthood for God. Paul will speak of the Christian body as the "Israel of God" in Galatians 6:16 or the "circumcision" in Philippians 3:3–4. The author of Hebrews affirms the Christians' honor as the household of God, part of that same household within which Moses functioned as a faithful servant, and over which Jesus now stands as Son and "heir of all things" (Heb. 1:2; 3:1–6).

Perhaps the richest assortment of titles applied to (largely Gentile) Christian communities is to be found in 1 Peter. The author begins by calling the believers the "resident aliens" living in the "Diaspora" (1 Pet. 1:1–2; NRSV calls them "exiles of the dispersion"), which was a term used by Jews to describe their existence as a people scattered throughout the nations. Now the term is applied by the author of 1 Peter to the early church, calling the believers' attention to their unity as a special and distinctive people, even though they exist as small communities scattered throughout the eastern provinces of the Mediterranean. Just as many Jews regarded their hearts' home as Jerusalem rather than the Gentile city in which they happened to reside (e.g., Rome or Antioch), so now the Christians are invited to regard themselves as "foreigners" living in what was formerly their native country, with their hearts' home in the kingdom of God, which they begin to experience in the "household" of the church.

The author of 1 Peter goes on to affirm the honor and worth of the believers in God's eyes (even as believers are censured and abused by their non-Christian neighbors, who seek to correct the Christians' "deviant" way of life) with an accumulation of titles formerly applied to Israel:

> You are a chosen race, a royal priesthood, a holy nation, God's own people, in order that you may proclaim the mighty acts of him who called you out of darkness into his marvelous light. Once you were not a people, but now you are God's people; once you had not received mercy, but now you have received mercy. (1 Pet. 2:9–10)

The titles "chosen race," "royal priesthood," "holy nation," and "treasured possession" ("God's own people" reads in the Greek, more woodenly, "a people for a possession") recontextualize phrases from Exodus 19:6 and Deuteronomy 7:6, bringing together in one place the titles that lie at the heart of Jewish identity and ethnic pride. "God's own people" also recalls Isaiah 43:21, where God calls Israel "the people whom I formed for myself so that they might declare my praise." These titles are now ascribed to the church as a means to provide it with a sense of its own value in God's sight (as a counterpart to ethnic pride) as well as to begin to articulate the ethos of this group (e.g., a group that maintains "holiness" suited to God's own people and that has the honor of God as the goal of its existence). The reader recognizes as well the incorporation of Hosea 2:23 (seen above in Rom. 9:24–26), again applied to a largely Gentile Christian readership.

Prior to this accumulation of titles, the author of 1 Peter uses the images of temple and priesthood—two realities that stood at the heart of Israelite religion and two symbols that were central to its identity as a people of God—to give shape to the believers' view of themselves:

> Come to him, a living stone, though rejected by mortals yet chosen and precious in God's sight, and like living stones, let yourselves be built into a spiritual house, to be a holy priesthood, to offer spiritual sacrifices acceptable to God through Jesus Christ. For it stands in scripture: "See, I am laying in Zion a stone, a cornerstone chosen and precious; and whoever believes in him will not be put to shame." (1 Pet. 2:4–6)

The community of disciples is invited to regard itself as a temple, made not with stones and mortar but with their own persons coming together into a worshiping body. The believers are also invited to regard themselves as the priesthood officiating in this "spiritual" temple, offering not animal sacrifices but "spiritual" sacrifices (here left undefined, perhaps so as to include the whole of their communal experience). As in Acts 3 and Galatians 3, 1 Peter also claims a new basis for the formation of this people of God, namely, being joined to Christ, the cornerstone, who becomes the defining center of the people of God and guarantor that honor will come to the group and dishonor to its opponents (see 1 Pet. 2:7–8). Those who trip over this stone rather than fit themselves to it are excluded from the building.

We may also observe at this point how the emphasis laid by New Testament authors on (1) the redefinition of who makes up "Israel" or the "descendants/heirs of Abraham" and (2) the Old Testament's vision of a single congregation of Jews and Gentiles worshiping the One God serves to legitimate the new community and its place in God's plan. The fact that the church quickly became a largely Gentile phenomenon, its message rejected by the majority of the Jewish people, called into question its legitimacy as heir to the promises of Abraham and to the titles that had belonged to Israel. By drawing on these resources from within the Jewish tradition, however, the authors of the New Testament (and the many church leaders who would have used these resources in similar manner) were able to develop lines of continuity and put to rest any doubts entertained within the community (or answer any challenges posed from outside) concerning the church's place in God's ongoing formation of a people for God's own possession.

The mixed Christian body of Jews and Gentiles can, from this vantage point, continue to read the Hebrew Scriptures as their own sacred history and look to that sacred history for moral instruction within the new community (see 1 Cor. 10:1–13; Heb. 3:7–19; 11:1–40). The authors of the New Testament go so far as to see a repetition of the sacred history of Israel in the church's present and forthcoming experience. In Jesus' death, they have experienced a new Passover (1 Cor. 5:7–8) and are currently called to a new exodus and a new entry into a promised land (Heb. 4:1–11; 13:12–14). These motifs figure prominently in Revelation, wherein the plagues of Egypt fall now on the whole unbelieving world for its idolatries, while the faithful are "sealed" by God so that they will not be harmed by these plagues (Rev. 7:1–3; 8–9; 16), and they sing a song of deliverance by another sea (Rev. 15:2–4; cf. Ex. 15).

Because both church and synagogue laid claim to the same scriptures, each one understanding itself to represent the group in true continuity with God's historic people, there was a high degree of tension between Christians and (non-Christian) Jews. The early Christians needed reassurance of their own legitimate place in God's people in the face of competing and conflicting understandings of the scriptures, and their leaders often provided this in the form of "disinheriting" the non-Christian Jews.

Striking in this regard is a Jesus saying preserved in Matthew. After encountering the Roman centurion whose certainty in Jesus' ability to confer divine favors is absolute, Jesus remarks,

> "Truly I tell you, in no one in Israel have I found such faith. I tell you, many will come from east and west and will eat with Abraham and Isaac and Jacob in the kingdom of heaven, while the heirs of the kingdom will be thrown into the outer darkness, where there will be weeping and gnashing of teeth." (Mt. 8:10–12)

Jesus' saying envisions here not only the inclusion of Gentiles at God's eschatological banquet because of their positive response to God, but the exclusion of many Jews from that very banquet that was popularly believed to be their birthright. As this is read in the early church, it would appear to exclude the possibility of the non-Christian Jewish community standing in continuity with the historic people of God—their own ancestors—alongside the Christian community. A similar impression is made in Acts 13:44–49. After Paul's proclamation of Jesus as Messiah is rejected by the Jewish people of Antioch, Paul and Barnabas declare, "It was necessary that the word of God should be spoken first to you. Since you reject it and judge yourselves to be unworthy of eternal life, we are now turning to the Gentiles" (Acts 13:46). As in Acts 3:17–26 (see above), rejection of the message about Jesus means exclusion from the company of the heirs of Abraham.

Perhaps the most poignant statement of this theme appears in Galatians 4:21–31, Paul's rewriting of the genealogical lines of church and synagogue:

> Abraham had two sons, one by a slave woman and the other by a free woman. One, the child of the slave, was born according to the flesh; the other, the child of the free woman, was born through the promise. Now this is an allegory: these women are two covenants. One woman, in fact, is Hagar, from Mount Sinai, bearing children for slavery. Now Hagar is Mount Sinai in Arabia and corresponds to the present Jerusalem, for she is in slavery with her children. But the other woman corresponds to the Jerusalem above; she is free, and she is our mother…Now you, my friends, are children of the promise, like Isaac. But just as at that time the child who was born according to the flesh persecuted the child who was born according to the Spirit, so it is now also. But what does the scripture say? "Drive out the slave and her child; for *the child of the slave will not share the inheritance with the child of the free woman.*" (Gal. 4:22–26, 28–30; emphasis mine)

By emphasizing "flesh" and "promise," connecting the former with the requirement of circumcision and the latter with the requirement of trust in God's promise, Paul is able to cross the natural lines of descent here. It is no longer physical descent that links one to Isaac, but being born into God's family by means of faith in God's promise, with the result that only Christian Jews and Christian Gentiles are accounted Isaac's descendants, while the majority of Isaac's natural descendants (the non-Christian Jews and Judaizing Christians) are now accounted children of Hagar, the slave woman. The very scripture that had formerly privileged the Jewish people over the descendants of Ishmael (Hagar's son; see Gen. 21:10) is now quoted to disinherit the non-Christian Jews. According to this ideological reading of the Genesis story, the Christian community has, in essence, supplanted the Jewish people in terms of their spiritual birthright.

In our contemporary context, and particularly in the wake of the extremes of anti-Judaism manifested in the Holocaust, many Christians are increasingly uncomfortable with the hostility between non-Christian Jew and Christian in the New Testament writings. In this climate, Paul's own deep, painful wrestling in Romans 9–11 with the question of the place in God's plan of those Jews who persist in rejecting Jesus becomes especially important for shaping a Christian response to the Jewish people. This response continues to hold on to hope for the future of the Jewish people in God's redemption story and to respond to Jews out of that passion and love, rather than as rivals or write-offs.

Although he begins his discussion of Israel's continued place in God's plan by invoking the remnant themes of the Old Testament, seemingly content to leave the bulk of ethnic Israel cut off from God's "Israel" (Rom. 9:6–13, 27–29), Paul cannot in the end keep God's faithfulness to God's special people from returning to his mind. God's preservation of a remnant within Israel of Jews who have responded positively to God's Messiah is offered as a sign that God has not rejected God's historic people (Rom. 11:1–6). Indeed, Paul perceives God's own hand at work in the widespread Jewish rejection of Jesus as Messiah. Israel's cutting off of itself from the people of God has made room for the Gentiles to join themselves to God's people (Rom. 11:17–24): "Through their stumbling salvation has come to the Gentiles" (Rom. 11:11).

This does not give Gentiles cause to boast over against the Jewish people (just as Paul had earlier argued that their privileges in God's plan did not give the Jews ground for boasting over against the Gentiles). Rather, the Gentile Christians must simply stand in awe of God's mercy and kindness toward them. In God's plan, both the disobedient Gentile, who refused God's claim to exclusive worship and obedience, and the disobedient Jew, who rejected God's Messiah and God's desire to include the Gentiles in his people by this means, receive God's mercy. Because both consign themselves to disobedience and receive God's favor at that point of disobedience, there will be unity and equal standing of the two in God's final drawing together of the people of God (11:26–32). Paul holds on firmly to the hope that those Jews who have rejected God's new movement in the world through Jesus and the Spirit will themselves fall in line with that movement in the end: "If their stumbling means riches for the world, and if their defeat means riches for Gentiles, how much more will their full inclusion mean!...If their rejection is the reconciliation of the world, what will their acceptance be but life from the dead!" (Rom. 11:12, 15). Both continue to be inseparably intertwined in God's plan of redemption of the one, whole humanity, the final acts of which are yet to be played out on history's stage.

The Ethos of the Christian Community

A second major concern of the early church leaders who authored the New Testament is the fostering of a distinctive group ethos that would sustain the commitment of individual believers over time. By *ethos* I mean the collective set of affects, attitudes, and commitments that gives membership in the group a distinctive "flavor" or character, and that guides members within the group to respond to one another in specific ways. A great deal of the New Testament is given over to this topic, whether in positively promoting and shaping this ethos or in defending it against encroachments of the ethos of the dominant culture—the ethos into which its members had been socialized from birth and thus one that was to be eliminated from the Christian community only with persistence and effort.

A major resource for the formation of Christian ethos is the promotion of the community as one's primary kin group, together with acceptance of the obligations of kin—chiefly of brothers and sisters—toward one another. The community of disciples was first and foremost the household of God, the "family of faith" (Gal. 6:10). As sons and daughters of One Parent (Jn. 1:12–13), born into a new family, inheritance, and destiny (1 Pet. 1:3–4, 18, 23–25), the Christians become brothers and sisters to one another. The formation of this community as a "fictive kinship group," that is, a group of people who are unrelated by blood but who nevertheless regard one another and act toward one another as kin, is rooted in the expanded definition of family that Jesus teaches in Matthew 12:50: "Whoever does the will of my Father in heaven is my brother and sister and mother." Moreover, the disciple who has been rejected by his or her natural family inherits a much larger family in the community of disciples: "There is no one who has left house or brothers or sisters or mother or father or children or fields, for my sake and for the sake of the good news, who will not receive a hundredfold now in this age—houses, brothers and sisters, mothers and children, and fields" (Mk. 10:29–30).

Throughout the New Testament writings, believers are most frequently addressed and referred to as "brothers and sisters" (the NRSV unfortunately obscures this by rendering the Greek "brothers" as "beloved" or "believers" or "friends"). Each Christian is thus repeatedly and consistently invited to regard fellow believers as the closest of kin and to respond to them from that basis. The recurring watchword for the ethos of the group is *philadelphia*, "brotherly and sisterly love" (Rom. 12:10; 1 Thess. 4:9; Heb. 13:1; 1 Pet. 1:22; 3:8). It is this quality that is to characterize the community of believers. Even where the word itself is not used, its several attributes are, as becomes clear once one immerses oneself in the context of Greco-Roman ethical discussions about how kin should behave. Antiquity has left us several rich discussions of this topic, notably Plutarch's essay "On Brotherly Affection" and some segments of Aristotle's *Nicomachean Ethics*. The following synopsis draws mainly from these sources, although most of the elements of the sibling ethic can be found in other Jewish and Greco-Roman texts as well.

First, kin (especially siblings) were expected to cooperate with one another in every way, each seeking how to assist the other in achieving what was beneficial. Competition and rivalry between siblings, however acceptable and "natural" Americans might view it, were regarded as shameful and to be avoided at all costs. Better to lose a quarrel, to lose face, or to lose a larger share of an inheritance than to lose the unity and harmony that should exist between siblings. Siblings were directed to seek how they might indulge one another rather than claim victories over one another, to share in one another's honors and advantages rather than compete and boast against one another. For siblings to try to hinder one another's pursuits was regarded as unnatural as for one foot to trip up the other as a person walked.

Harmony, unity, and concord were to be the hallmarks of sibling relationships. Brothers and sisters were called to share a common commitment to a noble way of life, prefer agreement and concord to dissent and self-assertion, and look out for one another's interests. This harmony was especially to manifest itself in their use of possessions. The division of an inheritance could pose a great threat to the harmony of siblings; moralists emphasized that one actually came out the poorer if one fought with a sibling over an inheritance and won a greater share of the property but lost the heart of the sibling. Instead, siblings were to regard their possessions as a common inheritance, to be used in common even though it was divided up among different stewards and caretakers. Wherever harmony was breached by offenses against one another, the offending sibling was urged to admit the wrong quickly and seek forgiveness, the offended sibling gently to point out the offense and quickly to offer forgiveness. Family disagreements were not to become public matters, lest the honor of the family be besmirched by this display of disharmony. Indeed, the offenses and shame of one's siblings or kin were to be hidden from the outside world if at all possible. There was nothing to be gained by parading a sibling's failure or dishonorable actions. Rather, reconciliation was to be speedily sought and speedily accomplished within the family so that harmony would be restored.

The New Testament authors use these guidelines for sibling relationships in their own formation of Christian communities and interpersonal relations within the churches. Mutual love is held up everywhere as the hallmark of the Christian group (e.g.,

Jn. 13:34–35; 15:12–13; Rom. 12:9–10, 15–16; 13:8–10; 1 Thess. 4:9–10; 1 Pet. 1:22; 3:8; 1 Jn. 2:7–11; 3:16–18; 4:7–12; 5:1; 2 Jn. 5–6). This love manifests itself in practical terms in the same ways that "sibling love" is expected to manifest itself. First, this love entails a commitment to sharing possessions, to putting one's own personal and material resources at the disposal of sisters and brothers in need (Acts 4:32–35; Gal. 6:9–10; Heb. 6:9–12; 13:16; 1 Jn. 3:16–18). Love also manifests itself as one sister or brother assiduously avoids what could injure a sibling. Paul's prohibitions of exercising one's freedoms in a way that would entice another believer to sin against his or her own conscience, for example, lead in this direction (e.g., 1 Cor. 8). Rather than insisting on having one's own way at the cost of a brother or sister's well-being, the loving sibling will forgo his or her rights in order to safeguard the well-being of the other. Far from hindering another's progress in the gospel, each believer is charged with keeping his or her fellow believers on the right track (see Heb. 3:13; 10:24–25; 12:15–17), cooperating in the great joint venture of pursuing their divine inheritance together.

Moreover, Christians are urged to "bear with one another and, if anyone has a complaint against another, forgive each other" (Col. 3:13). The same gentleness (Gal. 6:1), patience, and speed to become reconciled that one observes between honorable kin is to be observed in the family of God. In all speech and interaction, the bond between believers is to be maintained and used as the guiding principle to one's tone and intentions: "Do not speak harshly to an older man, but speak to him as to a father, to younger men as brothers, to older women as mothers, to younger women as sisters—with absolute purity" (1 Tim. 5:1–2).

Given the competitive nature of the Greco-Roman environment, in which non-kin were accustomed to compete with one another for precedence, power, influence, and other limited resources, it is perhaps not surprising to find the New Testament authors frequently engaged in defusing tendencies toward factionalism and competition and rerouting these energies toward cooperation and the maintenance of the bond of unity. The value of unity and cohesion within the group is clearly articulated by the idealized portrait of the earliest Christian community in Acts 2 and 4: "Now the whole group of those who believed were of one heart and soul, and no one claimed private ownership of any possessions" (Acts 4:32). It is to this ideal that the authors of the New Testament were continually calling their congregations, because such harmony and cooperation were often jeopardized by the tendency toward competition, self-promotion, and jockeying for precedence over one another in the court of public opinion.

Paul's letter to the Christians in Philippi, a church that had supported Paul spiritually, relationally, and materially through some difficult times in the apostle's career, offers a window into the importance of maintaining the bond of unity within a congregation. There are few direct clues concerning the situation of this church, but the vehemence of Paul's appeal to seek unity and put aside whatever makes for division (1:27–2:14) suggests that the one disagreement he does specifically name was a rather disruptive one: "I urge Euodia and I urge Syntyche to be of the same mind in the Lord. Yes, and I ask you also, my loyal companion [or loyal Syzygus], help these women, for they have struggled beside me in the work of the gospel" (4:2–3). Paul may thus be building throughout his letter toward this direct exhortation concerning a rift in the church between two important church leaders who perhaps have lost sight of their common venture and allowed disagreement, self-seeking, pressing one's own agenda in the church, or the desire for precedence and recognition to erode the unity of the whole group.

Paul reminds these leaders, and indeed the whole church, that they are engaged in a struggle against a hostile society that would seek to dissolve the church, and so they cannot afford factions and divisions inside as well (1:27–28). They need to pool all their strength to withstand the pressures already on them from outside the church and from certain threats within the church (such as the Judaizers, whose existence is again used as a call to focus the church on a common enemy in order to speed reconciliation within the church; 3:2–3). More essential, however, is the basic incompatibility between the self-seeking that gives rise to friction and eventually rifts in relationships and the example of Jesus that stands at the heart of the church's confession:

> If then there is any encouragement in Christ, any consolation from love, any sharing in the Spirit, any compassion and sympathy, make my joy complete: be of the same mind, having the same love, being in full accord and of one mind. Do nothing from selfish ambition or conceit, but in humility regard others as better than yourselves. Let each of you look not to your own interests, but to the interests of others. Let the same mind be in you that was in Christ Jesus, who, though he was in the form of God, did not regard equality with God as something to be exploited, but emptied himself, taking the form of a slave, being born in human likeness. And being found in human form, he humbled himself and became obedient to the point of death—even death on a cross. (Phil. 2:1–8)

Just as Jesus set aside any self-promoting agenda and any attempt to insist on recognition, so the disciples of Jesus are called on to adopt the same attitude in their life together as a community. The *ekklesia,* the "assembly," has been called out from such worldly, self-seeking patterns of relationship and called to be other-centered, more interested in bestowing honor and in affirming the worth and importance of fellow believers than in claiming honor or demanding recognition. Such an attitude can indeed engender a strong, united community. It is noteworthy that Paul understands "being of one mind" to result from the disciples' shared experience of God's spirit, encouragement, and love. It derives not from complete agreement about doctrine, practice, or church organization. Rather, a diversity of opinion regarding such matters is to be tolerated for the sake of maintaining firm the bond of unity and love (see especially Rom. 14:1–15:7).

Paul's letters to the Corinthian Christians also provide a rich study of how the ethos of kinship within the church must replace the tendencies learned from the dominant culture toward factionalism, divisiveness, and competition for precedence. Paul identifies these at the start of his first letter as the chief problems in Corinth: "I appeal to you, brothers and sisters…that all of you be in agreement and that there be no divisions among you, but that you be united in the same mind and the same purpose" (1 Cor. 1:10). Factions had grown up within the church over which apostle or teacher was the best endowed or most skilled (much as fans of rival sport teams or athletic heroes argue today; see 1 Cor. 1:10–13; 3:1–9; 4:1–7). Those Christians who had no scruples about eating food that had been sacrificed to idols were looking down on, and claiming a greater spiritual maturity and freedom than, their sisters and brothers who avoided such foods as polluting (1 Cor. 8; 10). Even spiritual gifts such as speaking in tongues and prophesying became causes for boasting over fellow believers (1 Cor. 12; 14).

Paul seeks to remedy this situation by stressing two basic facts about Christian community. First, all the positive growth or activity within the church is evidence of God's gifting and generosity, not a product of human skill or achievement and hence no cause for claiming precedence over one another (1 Cor. 4:7). Second, the community of disciples as a whole is not a collection of individuals but a single, living organism, a single "body" that God is bringing together, nourishing, and growing (1 Cor. 12:12–31). This metaphor, in which all the believers are viewed as parts of a single, living organism, articulates the pinnacle of harmony and cooperation. The individual believers are all God's gifts for one another, each one contributing something essential to the resources needed by the whole and by every other member for the whole to succeed:

> Just as the body is one and has many members, and all the members of the body, though many, are one body, so it is with Christ…If the foot would say, "Because I am not a hand, I do not belong to the body," that would not make it any less a part of the body…If the whole body were an eye, where would the hearing be? If the whole body were hearing, where would the sense of smell be?…The eye cannot say to the hand, "I have no need of you," nor again the head to the feet, "I have no need of you." On the contrary, the members of the body that seem to be weaker are indispensable, and those members

> of the body that we think less honorable we clothe with greater honor, and our less respectable members are treated with greater respect; whereas our more respectable members do not need this. But God has so arranged the body, giving the greater honor to the inferior member, that there may be no dissension within the body, but the members may have the same care for one another. If one member suffers, all suffer together with it; if one member is honored, all rejoice together with it. (1 Cor. 12:12, 15, 17, 21–26)

In this brief paragraph, Paul is able to take several causes of division and criteria of in-group ranking and turn them into sources of unity and cooperation. First, he establishes the importance of diversity within the body, so that the many necessary functions of a living community may all be fulfilled. The identity of one believer or group of believers can never become the standard by which another individual can be said to "belong" or "not belong" to the group. Belonging in the body of Christ (the church) can never be decided on the basis of looking like the other believers or some subset thereof. Without diversity, the body would be incomplete, partial, deformed.

Second, Paul emphasizes the indispensability of each of these diverse members, such that no one part or group of parts can rightfully say that another part is unnecessary. Instead, each part must value positively every other part as a necessary contributor to the range of functions that must be performed for the life of the whole body. Contrary to the way people treat each other in the non-Christian culture, despising the weak and scorning the less presentable persons in their midst, the community of disciples is to treat the weaker members of the body with greater care and respect, bestowing more honor and respect on those less naturally endowed so that there will indeed be a sense of oneness, of common commitment to one another, and of harmony. Paul's vision for community continues to challenge Christian communities (see Rom. 12:4–8; 1 Cor. 12:4–26; 14:1–5; Eph. 4:7, 11–13; 1 Pet. 4:8–11).

Another important aspect of community ethos, besides the development of a kinship ethic within the church, is the emphasis placed by New Testament authors on valuing and affirming fellow group members based on what gives them worth in God's sight rather than in the eyes of the larger world. The first-century world was highly stratified in terms of socioeconomic lines (in this regard it differs little from the modern world), and people were valued and honored proportionately. One place where this appears in the New Testament is in Paul's admonitions concerning the celebration of the Lord's supper (in conjunction, it would appear, with a love feast or "Agape Meal") in Corinth, where the patrons would begin early and entertain each other with a lavish feast while reserving the common elements of bread and wine and simple fare for the day laborers who would come to the meeting at the end of the workday (1 Cor. 11:17–34). Such a practice was thoroughly in keeping with the social expectations of Greco-Roman culture, in which banquet servers would allocate different portions and qualities of food proportionate to the social standing of each guest. Nevertheless, it was not in keeping with the ethos of Christian culture, in which all are brought to the table as sisters and brothers—members sharing equally in the honor of the one family of God. Paul therefore insisted that gatherings of the community of disciples reflect this Christian valuing of each member, rather than replicating the social hierarchies that had value in the world that was passing away (see also Jas. 2:1–7).

In addition to social classes, other barriers to unity were to be put away within the new community: "As many of you as were baptized into Christ have clothed yourselves with Christ. There is no longer Jew or Greek, there is no longer slave or free, there is no longer male and female; for all of you are one in Christ Jesus" (Gal. 3:27–28). The dividing wall of hostility between Jew and Gentile was thus eliminated by Jesus' death for all (see Eph. 2:11–22), and this new state of affairs was to be modeled within the new community, wherein Jewish Christian and Gentile Christian welcomed each other as equal partners in a heavenward calling (Rom. 15:7–12).

Similarly, the caste division of slave and free person would no longer be a meaningful division of humanity within the community of disciples. This comes out most poignantly in Paul's letter to Philemon, a householder in Colossae whose discontented slave ran away to Paul for mediation and came to be converted by Paul: "Perhaps this is the reason he was separated from you for a while, so that you might have him back forever, no longer as a slave but more than a slave, a beloved brother–especially to me but how much more to you, both in the flesh and in the Lord" (Philem. 15–16). Philemon can no longer treat Onesimus as a slave, as someone "foreign" and "other" in some sense, but as an equal (if somewhat junior) member of the family of God. It is this relationship that is to guide their future interactions, rather than the "worldly" relationship of indignant master to dissatisfying and dissatisfied slave.

The same would be true of other roles and relationships within the Christian household. The dominant culture's subordination of women to men in the household (although many philosophers argued for mutual kindness and gentleness, not countenancing tyranny on the male's part) is modified by the relationship of man and woman in the family of God. Although the husband's authority is not removed, it is now to be exercised as Jesus exercised his authority, namely in serving and seeking the welfare of the other, and thus submission becomes a two-way street (Eph. 5:21–30). The wife has become the "fellow heir of the gracious gift of life" and therefore worthy of the husband's honor (1 Pet. 3:7; au. trans.; the NRSV unfortunately obscures this connection). Gender no longer gives one partner a superior status or honor, but the equality of siblings (fellow heirs) comes to the fore instead.

This redefinition of how one values other human beings (particularly fellow disciples) extends to all criteria by which members of the non-Christian society evaluate and rank themselves and one another. In Paul's second letter to the Christians in Corinth, the apostle especially writes against the tendency–still so prominent in Western culture–to evaluate people on the basis of appearances and ascribe worth on that basis. The believers in that bustling urban center were prone from the beginning to value impressive appearance, eloquent speech, flashy spiritual endowments, and the like, evaluating and promoting their favorite apostles and teachers by such criteria. They appear to have been easy prey for certain Christian teachers who could play up to their admiration for smooth presentation and worldly credentials, and some teachers tried to replace Paul in the hearts of the Corinthian believers by just such an approach.

Paul devotes a large portion of his second letter to explaining why visible appearances and worldly credentials are an unreliable foundation for building up one's own sense of honor and worth and for evaluating another's worth (see 2 Cor. 1:3–9; 3:17–18; 4:7–5:12; 12:7b–10; 13:4). The flesh—here denoting human strengths and the appeal of physical appearances and observable endowments—is passing away along with the rest of the material creation (see chapter 4 below) and so cannot provide any adequate measure of ultimate worth. All worldly, fleshly strengths are weakness in the face of death and decay. The only thing that actually gives a person real, lasting strength is the Spirit of God at work within, transforming the person into the image of Jesus and delivering the person from this realm of death into God's eternal realm (see also Phil. 3:4–14). Paul points to his own weaknesses as the place where he boasts, for in his weaknesses the power of God at work is most transparent. Only God's power can transform the human being and save one from the grave, so only that power at work in a human being has value. All the flashy appearances and polished performances are merely attempts to mask the fading nature of human weakness and mortality, and they end up preventing people (both the performer and the onlookers) from encountering that one life-changing power that really matters. Paul censures measuring oneself against other people, and trying to establish one's own self-worth and status by such comparison, as foolishness (2 Cor. 10:12), urging the disciples instead to keep their eyes ever on that one standard, namely Jesus, and to value one another based on God's inner, unseen work.

Alongside an ethic shaped by the ideal of sisters and brothers, "holiness" continues to exercise a profound effect on shaping the community of disciples, just as it had enjoyed (and continued to enjoy) a profound effect on the shaping of the Jewish community. The holiness of God, one will recall, was to be reflected in the holiness of God's people. Both Jews and Gentiles were familiar with "holy" and "common," "clean" and "unclean" as meaningful categories. What was "holy" was set apart from ordinary use ("common") as a divinity's special possession or for service to that divinity. Just as the "holy" was surrounded with a sense of power for the benefit of the community (but also for its harm should that holiness be presumed upon or threatened by uncleanness), so the "unclean" was also surrounded with a sense of negative power, of threat to the wholeness and well-being of the community. The early church leaders regarded the church as holy, a body of people set apart by God for special interaction with God and for God's special possession (see Rom. 1:7; 1 Cor. 3:17; Eph. 1:4; 1 Pet. 1:15–16; 2:9–10). They could therefore focus the Christian's concern on preserving that holiness intact from the desecration of defilements (the pollution of unclean things), and indeed they capitalized on the basic cultural aversion to pollution as a means by which to maintain the community of faith and its distinctive faith and ethos.

The New Testament identifies three main sources of communal defilement (a complementary aspect to the holiness maintained by each believer, as discussed in chapter 2) against which the believers are called to guard. The first is the defilement of sin inside the community. The sanctity of the body of Christ is itself threatened by the sin of the individual Christian, who is a part of that body. The believers are to keep in mind the ramifications of sin for the holiness (and hence wholeness) of the community, and such considerations are to strengthen their resolve not to choose a polluting course of action (e.g., engaging in idolatry or extramarital intercourse, but also greed, envy, malice, and the like; see 1 Cor. 6:9–20; Eph. 5:3–11; 1 Thess. 4:3–8; Jas. 1:27; 1 Pet. 2:11). They are also to preserve the holiness of the community through the solemn expulsion of the member who willfully persists in sin and refuses to stop the defiling behavior (1 Cor. 5:9–13).

A second concern is the defilement of perverting the community's faith and practice by false teachers. The "corruption" of the group's ideology and ethos threatens its union with the holy God, with the result that those who innovate on the fundamental message about Christ (as in 1 John) or teach a way of life that tolerates the pollution of certain sinful practices (again, idolatry and sexual looseness frequently come to the fore, as in

Rev. 2:14–15, 20–23) are to be rejected as a defiling presence in the midst of the holy community (see 2 Jn. 7–11; Jude 3–16, 18–19; the image of "yeast" in Gal. 5:7–9).

Finally, defilement may come on the community through too close an association with, or assimilation into, the surrounding non-Christian society and the dissipation of Gentile culture. This polluted lifestyle characterized especially the Gentile convert's past:

> Fornicators, idolaters, adulterers, male prostitutes, sodomites, thieves, the greedy, drunkards, revilers, robbers–none of these will inherit the kingdom of God. And this is what some of you used to be. But you were washed, you were sanctified, you were justified in the name of the Lord Jesus Christ and in the Spirit of our God. (1 Cor. 6:9–11)

It was from these pollutions that the Christians had been "washed" and "sanctified"–two terms from the realm of ritual purification for the removal of pollution. This line of thinking sets up a boundary between the Christian and his or her past life, which is thus labeled as unclean, as well as between the Christian and those who continue to live the unconverted life (see 1 Pet. 4:1–6). Passages such as this one, then, serve powerfully to create and maintain group boundaries and keep those lines clear and intact (see also Eph. 4:17–24; 1 Thess. 5:6–11; Jas. 4:4; 1 Jn. 2:15–17; 5:21).

A passage that effectively captures all three aspects of defilement and the call to preserve holiness is 2 Corinthians 6:14–7:1:

> Do not be mismatched with unbelievers. For what partnership is there between righteousness and lawlessness? Or what fellowship is there between light and darkness? What agreement does Christ have with Beliar? Or what does a believer share with an unbeliever? What agreement has the temple of God with idols? For we are the temple of the living God; as God said, "I will live in them and walk among them, and I will be their God, and they shall be my people. Therefore come out

> from them, and be separate from them, says the Lord, and touch nothing unclean; then I will welcome you, and I will be your father, and you shall be my sons and daughters, says the Lord Almighty." Since we have these promises, beloved, let us cleanse ourselves from every defilement of body and of spirit, making holiness perfect in the fear of God.

The first verses use a series of incompatible pairs to suggest to the hearers that they look at their existence in the world by means of such dichotomies. Paul suggestively orients the readers to look at the world thus in black-and-white terms rather than with an eye to the grays that tend to blur group boundaries and distinctions. He ascribes to the Christian group the status of a holy dwelling for the holy God, among whom the holy God makes God's home–with the accompanying expectation that the community will maintain a holiness appropriate to the presence of such a God. In the immediate context of the letter, association with false teachers is the "mismating" (the unclean mixing of two separate species) to be avoided, but as the Old Testament quotations take over the discourse in 6:17–18, the hearers are invited to reinforce all boundaries between themselves and the unclean things that threaten them (both the false teachers and the world from which they have been separated and have been called to maintain separation). The passage closes with an exhortation to cleanse the community itself in light of these promises of God's nearness and paternity; "defilement of body and of spirit" recalls the disruptions of sin (from fornication to malice and rivalry), as well as the polluting influence of false teachers and the surrounding culture.

Our attention to holiness as New Testament authors construe and promote this value already moves us toward exploring the spectrum of responses toward the outside world fostered by various New Testament texts. As a holy, sanctified, chosen people gathered "from every tribe and language and people and nation" (Rev. 5:9), the church is already marked off as distinct and separate from the larger society around it. Maintenance of the group's boundaries–both those social boundaries that distinguish fellow Christian from non-Christian and those ideological boundaries that give the group its distinctive ethos and identity—becomes an essential part of the church's ongoing existence.

As the distinctiveness of the group's membership and its values comes to be recognized by the surrounding society, conflict between society and church results. The difference of values leads to tension between the groups (because the values prized by the dominant culture are questioned or redefined by the group), mutual antagonism (as both church and society offer criticisms and challenges to each other), and hostility (especially as the empowered group uses shame, assault, and other "persuasive" techniques to call the deviants back in line with the society's values). We find evidence of this hostility throughout the New Testament, though rarely in the form of lynching or official execution. Rather, the Christians' neighbors relied mainly on insult, shunning, prejudicial treatment, physical assault, manipulation of the legal system, imprisonment, and economic pressures (see Mt. 10:24–25; Lk. 6:22–23, 26; Heb. 10:32–34; 1 Pet. 2:12, 15; 3:16–22; 4:4, 14–16; Rev. 2:9–10) to make their disapproval of the Christian converts' new commitments known and felt, hoping by such means to shame them into a return to more "acceptable" values and practices (e.g., participation in the idolatrous rituals that surrounded and sheltered so much of Greco-Roman public life). Occasionally, however, society's rejection could be so vehement that it resulted in the death of the Christian "deviant" (as in Rev. 2:13), and this is certainly the direction in which the hostility moved in the second and third centuries.

Church leaders responded to this censure and hostility by seeking ways to insulate group members from these outside pressures. They taught the believers to regard such hostility as expected, even normal, particularly related to the "norm" of Christ's own experience in this world on the way to eternal honor in God's presence (see 1 Pet. 2:4–10; Heb. 12:1–3; 2:9–10). Just as Jesus was rejected by unbelievers and even subjected to the extreme of hostility, God vindicated him and gave him incomparable honor in God's kingdom. Those who call Jesus "Lord," therefore, should not expect to fare better in this world (see Mt. 10:24–25; Jn. 15:20–25). They also have the assurance, however, that as they persevere in their fidelity to God through

Jesus, they will also enjoy the same end as Jesus, namely, honor in God's court.

Indeed, New Testament authors frequently emphasize the importance of the opinion God has of believers and their actions: The wise person, according to them, always does what pleases God and results in God's approval, even if this means accepting human disapproval and even reproach and disgrace along the way (Jn. 5:44; 12:42–43; Acts 5:41; 2 Cor. 4:16–18; 5:9–10; 2 Thess. 1:6–12; Heb. 11:24–26; 1 Pet. 1:6–7; 4:13–14). The reason this is wise is, first, that God's opinion of one lasts forever, whereas worldly honor and disgrace last only for a while. A believer is also insulated against his or her neighbors' disapproval and censure by consideration of the dishonorable way of life in which the unbelievers themselves persist and of the unbelievers' alienation from the truth about the world in which they live. Wherever New Testament authors speak of the error, darkness, ignorance, or vice of outsiders, they are reminding the hearers that they should not allow the approval or disapproval of non-Christians to affect their decision to remain faithful to Jesus and the way of life to which he called them (see 1 Thess. 5:2–9 and 1 Pet. 4:1–6). The endurance of insult and hardship imposed by outsiders is even transformed into a badge of honor within the Christian group. It is a contest in which they courageously compete, refusing to give in, and a process by which they are trained and shaped for life in God's presence eternally (see Phil. 1:29; Heb. 12:1–11; 1 Pet. 1:6–7).

Finally, as a strong, nurturing, and supportive community of disciples is formed around them, it becomes less and less likely that converts will give in to the pressures from outside. The quality and importance of the loving and encouraging relationships within the group will make approval and acceptance by one's fellow believers more important than approval by members of the larger society. It is highly unlikely that the early church would have survived had the ethos of kinship not taken root, resulting in an astounding willingness on the part of members to share their resources to meet the needs of sisters and brothers, to stand by sisters and brothers who had been especially singled out by society for harsh treatment, and ultimately to put one another's well-being and continued perseverance in the race of faith ahead of one's own safety, amassing of wealth, and self-interest. Their commitment to one another in such real and costly ways stands as a poignant challenge to their spiritual descendants.

Despite the early church's interest in remaining separate and distinct from the society around them, and even in the face of ongoing reproach and opposition, the New Testament authors continue to orient the churches toward the conversion of outsiders to the group. This conversionist approach to the outside world is explicit in the command of Jesus to his disciples preserved at the close of Matthew's gospel (Mt. 28:19–20) and at the beginning of Acts (Acts 1:8), but it also appears in the early church's understanding that it was the vehicle by which God would fulfill the Old Testament's vision of a universal people of God. Jesus is the "light for revelation to the Gentiles" (Lk. 2:32; see Acts 13:47, which applies this also to Jesus' emissaries), the one in whose name all are called to return to God. The growth of the church is the outworking of the hope that "all other peoples may seek the Lord—even all the Gentiles over whom my name has been called" (Acts 15:17), an outworking visible in the efforts of people such as Paul, Epaphras, Peter, and Apollos.

As an aid to this conversionist agenda, the New Testament authors show a high interest in dispelling slander and displaying the moral integrity of the group to the outside world that rejects the group. The author of 1 Peter, for example, instructs congregations throughout the provinces in Asia Minor to be certain to live upright lives devoid of criminal activity and to fill their lives with acts of kindness and beneficence in order to disprove the slander leveled at the group by outsiders (see 1 Pet. 2:11–12, 15; 3:16; 4:14–16). It is important not only to him but also to the Pauline team that believers show the nobility of their way of life to outsiders, so that at least one barrier to conversion will be removed (namely, prejudice against the group as a subversive and vice-ridden movement; see 1 Thess. 4:11–12). It is within the context of this interest in "putting your best foot forward" toward the members of the dominant culture that we should read some of the "household codes" of the New Testament, the instructions given to Christians concerning how to behave in their domestic situations. Noteworthy in this regard is Titus 2:2–10:

> Encourage the young women to love their husbands, to love their children, to be self-controlled, chaste, good managers of the household, kind, being submissive to their husbands, *so that the word of God may not be discredited*...Show yourself in all respects a model of good works, and in your teaching show integrity, gravity, and sound speech that cannot be censured; *then any opponent will be put to shame, having nothing evil to say of us.* Tell slaves to be submissive to their masters and to give satisfaction in every respect; they are not to talk back, not to pilfer, but to show complete and perfect fidelity, *so that in everything they may be an ornament to the doctrine of God our Savior.* (Titus 2:4–5, 7–10, emphasis mine)

The italicized portions of the text show the pervasive concern with arousing the goodwill and dispelling the slander and opposition of nonbelievers by means of a way of life that would be regarded as virtuous by the standards of the Greco-Roman culture in matters that did not violate God's call to holy living. A similar emphasis undergirds 1 Timothy 6:1–2, which urges Christian slaves to show complete deference and obedience to their masters, "so that the name of God and the teaching [i.e., the gospel] may not be blasphemed," and 1 Peter 3:1–7, where Christian wives of unbelieving men are directed to behave as the "ideal wife," as the dominant culture would define it, in order to win over their husbands' goodwill to the Christian cause and perhaps even convert them. The early church appears to have chosen its battles very carefully (e.g., the avoidance of all idolatry) and to have attempted to demonstrate its essential uprightness (and potential harmony with dominant cultural values) in other areas of life.

The early church did not expect to change the world by converting people "one soul at a time." Rather, they awaited God's intervention in the world and called people to join their community as the place of favor and safety in preparation for the great reversal that God would effect in the (near) future. The New Testament authors thus also nurtured a revolutionist response to the world around the church, one that called not for violent participation in the overthrow of that world order (as did the Zealot philosophy in Judea in the years leading up to the Jewish Revolt of 66–70 C.E.), but rather for fidelity to Jesus and to his call as the community waited for God to act in God's own time. So pervasive is this aspect of the community of disciples' orientation to the world around them that it will be treated at far greater length in chapter 4 (see Mk. 13; Heb. 10:36–39; 12:25–29; Rev. 11:15–18).

Life Together in the Christian Community

A staple of the believer's Christian experience was worshiping together with the gathered, local Christian community. The New Testament authors assume a regular assembling of the believers held in the houses of the propertied converts (see Rom. 16:3–5, 23; 1 Cor. 16:19; Philem. 1–2), probably on the first day of the week (Acts 20:7), as had come to be the norm already in the first half of the second century (*Epistle of Barnabas* 15; *Didache* 14; Justin, *First Apology* 67). The choice of this day as the communal day of worship is rather natural, given the emphasis in the community on the resurrection of Jesus as the signal of the inauguration of the age to come.

Acts and the Pauline literature provide the fullest descriptions within the New Testament of early Christian worship. The author of Acts portrays the earliest church as devoted to "the apostles' teaching and fellowship, to the breaking of bread and the prayers" (Acts 2:42). This "breaking of bread," which occurred in the homes of believers (Acts 2:46), involved the celebration of the Lord's supper (the eucharist) not just with bread and wine but also with the sharing of a full meal together (see *Didache* 9–10, which sets the eucharist in the context of a full meal). This is probably the context in which to understand Paul's complaint about the celebration of the Lord's supper in Corinth, preceded by a communal meal (called a "love-feast" in Jude 12). During that communal meal, the householder-patrons of the community would regale each other with fine and ample fare (even getting drunk with the excess of wine), while the poorer believers would be given sparse rations and leave hungry and humiliated (reminded by the "love-feast" of his or her poverty rather than of his or her honor in God's family). If the Lord's supper–the bread and the wine–are to be partaken of in a worthy manner, then the whole gathering must be conducted with decorum and in a way that honors rather than humiliates those believers of poorer means. This might be accomplished by a "love-feast" in which everyone is able to enjoy his or her fill without excess (as in *Didache* 10) or by abolishing all but the bread and wine. The purpose of the meal was to establish and increase the sense of unity among believers and unity with Christ, and any practice that hindered this purpose required correction.

The gathering of the believers was foremost a time of mutual encouragement, instruction, and communal experience of the power and proximity of the Spirit of God:

> What should be done then, my friends? When you come together, each one has a hymn, a lesson, a revelation, a tongue, or an interpretation. Let all things be done for building up. If anyone speaks in a tongue, let there be only two or at most three, and each in turn; and let one interpret. But if there is no one to interpret, let them be silent in church and speak to themselves and to God. Let two or three prophets speak, and let the others weigh what is said. If a revelation is made to someone else sitting nearby, let the first person be silent. For you can all prophesy one by one, so that all may learn and all be encouraged. And the spirits of prophets are subject to the prophets, for God is a God not of disorder but of peace. (1 Cor. 14:26–33)

> Let the word of Christ dwell in you richly; teach and admonish one another in all wisdom; and with gratitude in your hearts sing psalms, hymns, and spiritual songs to God. (Col. 3:16)

In the Pauline churches, at least, worship appears to have been characterized by an intense awareness of the Holy Spirit's leading and movement among the community. Each member, having this Spirit within, may be equipped to contribute something for the encouragement, instruction, and strengthening of fellow believers. The context of the passage from 1 Corinthians shows the potential for abuse of charismatic worship, namely, fixation on the gifts and on the claim to a special spiritual status that the more ecstatic gifts might be thought to confer. This misuse, however, does not nullify the value of such worship where the aim of mutual edification is kept humbly in view (1 Cor. 12:7; 14:12).

The early churches' awareness of the Spirit in the midst of their assemblies, manifested in the charismata (spiritual gifts) and other extraordinary phenomena, could not have failed to make a profound impact on the believers. What Paul hopes will be the visitor's response, namely, the profound awareness that "God is really among you" (1 Cor. 14:25), is also the impact of the experience on each participant. Encountering God and experiencing the Spirit's presence, guidance, and operation in the worshiping community provides a regular reminder for the believers that the course they have chosen in their conversion has brought them closer to God and has opened up resources for them richer than any they may have lost or will lose because of society's disapproval (or just from the diminished connections they enjoy in the world as a result of their avoidance of all idolatry). As in the grandiose vision of Revelation 4–5, the community of believers gathered around the One God and enjoying God's nearness is reminded that it has received accurate knowledge concerning the center of the cosmos and the One who rules the cosmos. This is perhaps the most important insulation believers can have against the censure and onslaughts of their neighbors.

This attitude of worship is to be carried by the believers through all their experiences individually and together throughout the week: "Be filled with the Spirit, as you sing psalms and hymns and spiritual songs among yourselves, singing and making melody to the Lord in your hearts, giving thanks to God the Father at all times and for everything in the name of our Lord Jesus Christ" (Eph. 5:18–20). The whole orientation of the believer's life is thus to be permeated with worship of God and the Lord Jesus—with internal and interpersonal reminders of the One who has called them to a new destiny and way of life, who has separated them from the unbelieving world and from their own past life by the waters of baptism, bringing them through those waters to a new hope, a new identity, and a new family (see the importance and meaning of baptism reflected in Rom. 6:1–11; Gal. 3:26–29; 1 Pet. 3:18–22).

If we permit ourselves to look just beyond the New Testament into the second-century Christian writings, we find that the reading of the Old Testament Scriptures as well as the "memoirs of the Apostles" constitutes a lengthy portion of the assembly—these are read, according to Justin, "as long as time permits" (*First Apology* 67). The reading is followed by an exhortation to live according to the teachings of those texts, the offering of prayers, and the celebration of the Lord's supper. This is also the occasion for "those who prosper" to contribute to the community's coffer (see 1 Cor. 16:1–4), from which the needs of the community, visitors, and others may be met.

Together with the other aspects of life together as a community, namely, mutual assistance and support in times of want (see 2 Cor. 8–9; Philem. 7; Heb. 6:9–12), solidarity in the face of outside pressure (Heb. 10:32–34), and keeping one another in line with the ethos and values of the family of God (e.g., 2 Thess. 3:6–15), the communal experience of worship was a powerful force in sustaining and shaping individual commitment and discipleship. Affirmed and energized by the manifestations of the Spirit, reminded of the community's love and partnership in the sharing of meals, instructed by the reading of scripture and by words of Christian prophets and teachers, the convert is continually made aware that he or she has become a part of the family of God and is enabled to persevere in the journey toward the eternal inheritance.

CHAPTER 4

Apocalypticism

The Triumph of God

A substantial, even surprising amount of the New Testament is devoted to describing and reinforcing the broader horizons of the Christian worldview, that is, how Christians are led to conceptualize the world around them and to understand "the way things work." A person's worldview has the potential to impact profoundly the way in which that person will live, as it provides a meaningful context for negotiating and interpreting the day-to-day experiences of life and for setting priorities and goals. The worldview promoted by, and assumed throughout, the New Testament is distinctly "apocalyptic." This means that the New Testament worldview looks beyond the everyday, observable world in terms of both time and space in order to create that meaningful framework for an individual's life and experience.

Apocalypticism is a label that has come to be attached to a number of strands of Jewish thought (as well as Greco-Roman, Persian, and Egyptian strands of thought) that share in common an interest in the activities that have been happening, are happening, and are yet to happen in unseen realms. These realms may include God's court, the places of punishment and reward prepared for human beings but not accessible now for inspection, the infernal regions, or the airy regions about us populated with mostly unseen inhabitants. "Apocalyptic" strands of thought also share an interest in that primeval history that set the world on its present course, as well as that final destiny toward which it is moving (or being moved, as by the supreme governance of God). The Christian thus finds himself or herself in the midst of a cosmic story with a beginning and an ending that can be known and can be invoked to explain the current state of affairs or to motivate pursuit of a certain course of action. He or she also discovers unseen inhabitants of an unseen world in conflict, whose power plays lie behind the visible machines of everyday experience. Awareness of the unseen players in the conflict can help the Christian discern the right side to be on in the visible world and the strategic course of action to pursue in order to hinder the enemy's advances and serve God's designs.

In this final chapter, we will explore the contours of the worldview promoted in the New Testament, the ways in which that worldview orients Christian readers toward the world in which they live, and the impact that such a worldview has on the early church's shaping of a distinctive ethos for itself. At the center of this worldview is the triumph of God—God's final subjugation of all spiritual and human opponents and establishment of a kingdom in which God's justice and God's values are fully evidenced.

"The Kingdom of God Is Near"

The focal point of the worldview promoted and shared by the New Testament authors is the kingdom of God. This is a point of continuity between the testaments, rooted in the conviction expressed frequently in the Psalms and Prophets of God's reign over the world God has created:

> The LORD has established his throne in the heavens, and his kingdom rules over all. (Ps. 103:19)
>
> Your kingdom is an everlasting kingdom, and your dominion endures throughout all generations. (Ps. 145:13)
>
> O LORD of hosts, God of Israel, who are enthroned above the cherubim, you are God, you alone, of all the kingdoms

> of the earth; you have made heaven and earth. (Isa. 37:16)
>
> Who would not fear you, O King of the nations? For that is your due. (Jer. 10:7)

The rule of God is especially manifest in the rise and fall of earthly kingdoms: To each God has allotted a certain time and place to rule, and each rules only for as long as it pleases God (Jer. 18:7–10).

This comes most forcefully to expression in the book of Daniel, in which the divine determination of the times and order of human kingdoms is a repeated theme: "The Most High is sovereign over the kingdom of mortals; he gives it to whom he will" (Dan. 4:17; see 4:25, 32; 5:21). This conviction is dramatically expressed in the episode of Belshazzar's feast, in which the handwriting on the wall spells out God's decree of a change of kingdoms: "This is the interpretation of the matter: MENE, God has numbered the days of your kingdom and brought it to an end;...PERES, your kingdom is divided and given to the Medes and Persians" (Dan. 5:26, 28). Within Daniel, however, the focus is on the kingdom that God will establish to replace all Gentile kingdoms, a kingdom in which God's rule will be directly evident:

> You, O king, the king of kings—to whom the God of heaven has given the kingdom, the power, the might, and the glory...After you shall arise another kingdom inferior to yours, and yet a third kingdom of bronze, which shall rule over the whole earth. And there shall be a fourth kingdom, strong as iron; just as iron crushes and smashes everything, it shall crush and shatter all these...And in the days of those kings the God of heaven will set up a kingdom that shall never be destroyed, nor shall this kingdom be left to another people. It shall crush all these kingdoms and bring them to an end, and it shall stand forever. (Dan. 2:37, 39–40, 44)

This kingdom of God, moreover, will elevate the people of God, the "saints" or "holy ones," to a position of favor and rule over the Gentile nations that formerly had exercised dominion over them:

> But the holy ones of the Most High shall receive the kingdom and possess the kingdom forever…Judgment was given for the holy ones of the Most High, and the time arrived when the holy ones gained possession of the kingdom…The kingship and dominion and the greatness of the kingdoms under the whole heaven shall be given to the people of the holy ones of the Most High; their kingdom shall be an everlasting kingdom, and all dominions shall serve and obey them. (Dan. 7:18, 22, 27)

In Daniel, the belief in God's sovereignty over human kingdoms takes on a distinctly apocalyptic color. God's sovereignty will manifest itself at some forthcoming time in God's elevation of God's own people to the position of reigning kingdom, reversing the normal political state of affairs that held during the exilic, postexilic, and Hellenistic periods. This kingdom of God will be unlike any human kingdom; the idyllic state of God reigning through God's people will not end.

The evangelists give the impression that there was widespread expectation among Palestinian Jews that God would bring in the kingdom that Daniel had described. Joseph of Arimathea is remembered as "a respected member of the council, who was also himself waiting expectantly for the kingdom of God" (Mk. 15:43). The crowds that greet Jesus as he marches into Jerusalem riding a donkey clearly interpret the event in terms of the hope that he is God's agent for freeing Israel from Roman domination and bringing back her glory as a sovereign state: "Blessed is the coming kingdom of our ancestor David! Hosanna in the highest heaven!" (Mk. 11:10). Many of the uprisings against Herodian and Roman rule were led by people claiming to be God's end-time agent, God's "anointed one" or "messiah," who would take back by force what had once belonged to Israel. It is thus small wonder that Jesus, who was hailed as the "anointed one," would be regarded as a potential agitator and leader of sedition by the Roman authorities.

It is this dynamic conception of human history giving way at some point to the kingdom of God that provides the backdrop for Jesus' preaching of the kingdom and the disciples' hearing and passing on of that message. "Proclaiming the good news of the kingdom" is a constant refrain heard throughout the synoptic gospels and Acts as a summary of the core message proclaimed first by Jesus and then by Jesus' witnesses (see Mt. 4:23; 9:35; 10:7; Acts 1:3; 8:12; 19:8; 20:25; 28:31). In Matthew's gospel, first John the Baptist, then Jesus, then the disciples issue this message:

> "Repent, for the kingdom of heaven has come near." (Mt. 3:2)
>
> From that time Jesus began to proclaim, "Repent, for the kingdom of heaven has come near." (Mt. 4:17)
>
> As you go, proclaim the good news, "The kingdom of heaven has come near." (Mt. 10:7)

The message is "good news" in that the kingdom of God is said to be "near," a welcome reversal that is immediately forthcoming and for which the people of God are to prepare through "repentance" and turning again to God with obedient hearts and lives. This was a distinctly "apocalyptic" message in that it called people to view themselves as living at the threshold of the new age, at the decisive break between the present order of Gentile domination and injustice and the forthcoming order of God's kingdom, "where righteousness is at home" (2 Pet. 3:13). It called people to respond in the present to the hope that God's end-time deliverance of God's people was near at hand. This positioning of humanity at the transition point from "ordinary history" to "God's kingdom" and eternal rule appears throughout the New Testament (see 1 Thess. 1:10; 4:15–18; Heb. 1:2; 9:26; 1 Pet. 1:3–5; 4:17–18; Rev. 22:6–7, 10, 12, 20), although with varying degrees of imminence.

Although Jesus' proclamation of this kingdom would be intelligible in terms of the apocalyptic hope shared (with great variations, of course) by many Palestinian Jews, Jesus also made clear that it was not to be a kingdom like those led by human authorities. When confronted with James and John's request to give them the highest positions of authority in his kingdom, Jesus responded by teaching that ideas of ranking and status were completely different in God's kingdom: "You know that among the Gentiles those whom they recognize as their rulers lord it over them, and their great ones are tyrants over them. But it is not so among you; but whoever wishes to become great among you must be your servant, and whoever wishes to be first among you must be slave of all" (Mk. 10:42–44; cf. Mt. 20:25–27). This teaching reinforces an earlier one spoken by Jesus: "Whoever becomes humble like this child is the greatest in the kingdom of heaven" (Mt. 18:4). Precedence in this world is a matter of domination and power over others, but in the kingdom it is a matter of pouring oneself out for others in love and service, imitating the example of the one who ushers in that kingdom, namely, Jesus.

Reflection on the qualities and nature of the kingdom of God invited reflection on the question of who would "inherit" the kingdom of God, that is, who would actually benefit from the coming of God's kingdom by being included in that kingdom. By means of this strategy, New Testament authors are able to use the apocalyptic hope to formulate and reinforce an ethos for the group based on the criterion of becoming worthy of God's kingdom. We see this already in Jesus' teaching on what constitutes honor and precedence in the kingdom above, and in the following passage, one observes how matching the character of the kingdom in one's own life becomes a prerequisite for entering that kingdom:

> At that time the disciples came to Jesus and asked, "Who is the greatest in the kingdom of heaven?"…and [Jesus] said, "Truly I tell you, unless you change and become like children, you will never enter the kingdom of heaven. Whoever becomes humble like this child is the greatest in the kingdom of heaven." (Mt 18:1–4)

Similarly, Jesus emphasizes the importance of obedience to God's will and God's commandments as the determining characteristic of those who would be a part of this kingdom:

> Not everyone who says to me, "Lord, Lord," will enter the kingdom of heaven, but only the one who does the will of my Father in heaven. (Mt. 7:21)
>
> Whoever breaks one of the least of these commandments, and teaches others to do the same, will be

> called least in the kingdom of heaven; but whoever does them and teaches them will be called great in the kingdom of heaven. For I tell you, unless your righteousness exceeds that of the scribes and Pharisees, you will never enter the kingdom of heaven. (Mt. 5:19–20)

Their obedient response to John the Baptist's call gives "the prostitutes and the tax collectors" a surer place in the kingdom of God than the religious elite, who fail to execute God's will from the heart (Mt. 21:31).

Jesus opposes any notion that descent from Abraham automatically means that one will be included in God's kingdom, as if that kingdom were merely a revival of the nation of Israel. He arouses bitter opposition with his redefinition of the heirs of the kingdom: "Many will come from east and west and will eat with Abraham and Isaac and Jacob in the kingdom of heaven, while the heirs of the kingdom will be thrown into the outer darkness, where there will be weeping and gnashing of teeth" (Mt. 8:11–12; cf. Lk. 13:28–29). Refusal to render to God the fruits God seeks leads to being excluded from that kingdom: "The kingdom of God will be taken away from you and given to a people that produces the fruits of the kingdom" (Mt. 21:43).

Wealth is regarded as a particular obstacle to entering the kingdom (see Mt. 19:16–24; Jas. 2:5), because being in God's kingdom means the sharing of resources with all who have need and not the privileging of oneself and one's own over all others that the amassing of wealth (while others go hungry) signifies. Instead, the ones who will hear the words "Come, you that are blessed by my Father, inherit the kingdom prepared for you from the foundation of the world" (Mt. 25:34) will be those who have lived out the kingdom values in this world—who have clothed and fed the poor, welcomed the stranger, visited the imprisoned, and cared for the sick (Mt. 25:31–46).

The leaders who nurtured the early church after Jesus' resurrection and ascension continued to develop this strategy. Paul, for example, vociferously affirms the need for righteous living and a break with one's sinful past in order to inherit the kingdom and enjoy a place in the age to come. Because "the kingdom of God is not food and drink but righteousness and peace and joy in the Holy Spirit" (Rom. 14:17), the church is to manifest those qualities in their life together rather than mar the community's peace and joy with arguments over permitted and forbidden food and drink. To those who attempt to enjoy the benefits of the coming kingdom while still indulging the passions of the fleshly nature, Paul writes,

> Do you not know that wrongdoers will not inherit the kingdom of God? Do not be deceived! Fornicators, idolaters, adulterers, male prostitutes, sodomites, thieves, the greedy, drunkards, revilers, robbers—none of these will inherit the kingdom of God. (1 Cor. 6:9–10)

> Now the works of the flesh are obvious: fornication, impurity, licentiousness, idolatry, sorcery, enmities, strife, jealousy, anger, quarrels, dissensions, factions, envy, drunkenness, carousing, and things like these. I am warning you, as I warned you before: those who do such things will not inherit the kingdom of God. (Gal. 5:19–21)

> Be sure of this, that no fornicator or impure person, or one who is greedy (that is, an idolater), has any inheritance in the kingdom of Christ and of God. (Eph. 5:5)

It thus becomes a primary agenda for the early Christians so to live as to be found worthy of the kingdom (see 1 Thess. 2:12; 2 Thess. 1:5) and to show by their obedience to God and their honorable response of gratitude to God (Heb. 12:28) and to Jesus that they belong to that kingdom rather than to this world, a world that, in its rebellion against God's lordship, is passing away. The apocalyptic transition from this age of corruption and sin to the coming age of righteousness becomes an ethical journey in the life of each believer: "He has given us...his precious and very great promises, so that through them you may escape from the corruption that is in the world because of lust, and may become participants of the divine nature" (2 Pet. 1:4). As they embody faithfulness, goodness, knowledge, self-control, endurance, godliness, brotherly and sisterly affection, and love, the believers are assured that "entry into the eternal kingdom of our Lord and Savior Jesus Christ will be richly provided for [them]" (2 Pet. 1:11; see 1:3–11).

Unlike the visions of Daniel, however, in which God's kingdom dramatically breaks into the human scene like the rock thrown from heaven to crush the last human kingdoms in Nebuchadnezzar's dream (see Dan. 2), Jesus proclaims a kingdom of God that is coming to the world in more subtle ways. To be sure, the kingdom's final manifestation will still be abrupt and definitive, as "the Son of Man will appear in heaven, and...all the tribes of the earth will mourn, and they will see 'the Son of Man coming on the clouds of heaven' with power and great glory" (Mt. 24:30). In language borrowed from Daniel (see Dan. 7:13), Jesus shares Daniel's vision of a dramatic breaking into the web of human history by God and God's agent. But Jesus also sees the kingdom of God as beginning to break in on this side of the day of the Lord. This introduces an "already" aspect to the Christian view of the end. The final resolution is "not yet" accomplished, but there are definite signs of its coming and even its presence "already" in the ministry of Jesus and the present experience of the believer.

Jesus describes the kingdom not only as "near" in the sense of "imminent" or "on the immediate horizon of history," but also as "near" in the sense of "present" among the people at the time of his ministry: "Once Jesus was asked by the Pharisees when the kingdom of God was coming, and he answered, 'The kingdom of God is not coming with things that can be observed; nor will they say, "Look, here it is!" or "There it is!" For, in fact, "the kingdom of God is among you"' (Lk. 17:20–21). The kingdom of God has already begun to dawn on the people, to intrude into the ordinary life of this age, the age of the kingdoms of this world. Although it will eventually break in like a mighty, crashing wave, it is already at work in this age. In a series of parables on the "kingdom of heaven" (Matthew's more common expression for the "kingdom of God"), Jesus describes the kingdom as "yeast that a woman took and mixed in with three measures of flour until all of it was leavened" (Mt. 13:33). The kingdom is something being planted in this present age, worked in and through the whole by God as a woman works the yeast into the whole lump of dough that she is making. When the kingdom arrives in all its fullness, it will be as the fruition of the leavening process that has already begun.

The New Testament authors understand Jesus' preaching, ministry, passion, and resurrection as signaling the beginning of the end of this age and the breaking in of the age to come. The doors of the kingdom of God were opened in John the Baptist's call to repent (Mt. 11:12), and all who responded were flocking into that kingdom. The presence of the kingdom is especially apparent, however, in the powerful ministry of Jesus, first in his driving back of the forces of the enemy who holds sway in the present age: "But if it is by the Spirit of God that I cast out demons, then the kingdom of God has come to you" (Mt. 12:28; see Lk. 11:20). There is also a close connection between Jesus' and the disciples' healing of the sick and the breaking in of God's kingdom. The former is a sign to the people of the reality of the latter (see Mt. 4:23; 9:35; Lk. 10:9).

Jesus' resurrection from the dead was seen as another sign of the last days. The resurrection of the dead (and the subsequent reward of the righteous) was a prominent feature in several Jewish groups' expectations for the end time, in which God would break in and establish God's kingdom. The resurrection of the one man, Jesus, was regarded by Paul as the "first fruits" (the first portion of the full harvest) of the general resurrection of all, and hence of the end of this age and the beginning of the next (see 1 Cor. 15:20–24). The time between the resurrection of Jesus and the resurrection of all is the time during which the two ages grind against each other, as it were, a time of upheavals and woes as the present order passes away and a new order comes into full being. During this in-between time, Jesus Christ is the focal point of the "new creation," and all who have joined themselves to Jesus in the mystical reality of his body, the church, are themselves part of this "new creation" (2 Cor. 5:16–17; Gal. 6:15), which still awaits the consummation in which all will be renewed.

Another signal to the early church leaders that the "last days" had been inaugurated was the believers' experience of the pouring out of the Holy Spirit, which Joel had identified as an end-time occurrence. Thus, when the apostles are filled with the Holy Spirit at Pentecost, Peter can interpret it as an eschatological sign:

> This is what was spoken through the prophet Joel: "In the last days it will be, God declares, that I will pour out my Spirit upon all flesh, and your sons and your daughters shall prophesy, and your young men shall see visions, and your old men shall dream dreams. Even upon my slaves, both men and women, in those days I will pour out my Spirit; and they shall prophesy." (Acts 2:16–18, quoting Joel 2:28–29)

Awareness of the Holy Spirit's dwelling in the midst of the congregation and even within each believer was a widespread characteristic of the early church as evidenced in the New Testament. This phenomenon, so close to each believer's own experience, could thus also be invoked as a sign of the breaking in of God's kingdom. The believers could be said to enjoy the Spirit of God as a "first fruits" of their full inheritance in God's kingdom (Rom. 8:14–17, 23), even as a "first installment" or "pledge" of the full inheritance that would soon be theirs (2 Cor. 1:22; 5:5; Eph. 1:13–14).

The Christian community, though it might be beleaguered and oppressed by the authorities of this age, is nevertheless itself already part of God's kingdom. The author of Colossians thus celebrates the deliverance effected by God for his people: "He has rescued us from the power of darkness and transferred us into the kingdom of his beloved Son" (Col. 1:13). Using language borrowed from Exodus 19:6, John also regards the community of the redeemed as "a kingdom, priests serving his God and Father" (Rev. 1:5–6; see also 5:9–10) established by Jesus through the ransom of his death. Living in the midst of this present age and still all too subject to its hostility, censure, and injustices, the community of disciples nevertheless "already" constitutes the kingdom of God. Enjoying this dignity in God's sight, it must nevertheless await the complete manifestation of this hidden kingdom in order to enjoy fully the goodness that God has prepared for its members. In the heavenly places, God's kingdom already exists (see Rev. 11:15; 12:10), but this fact is celebrated in celestial hymnody prior to its being worked out fully on the plane of human history.

It is this tension between the "already" and the "not yet" aspects of the kingdom of God that gives Christian apocalypticism its distinctive hue in the spectrum of early Jewish apocalyptic thought. While the end has been inaugurated and the kingdom rises in the midst of this age like yeast in dough–particularly in the experience and growth of the community of disciples–the future consummation of the kingdom's coming is never lost to view. Several texts specifically seek to prepare believers to endure a prolonged interim period (see, for example, the peculiar spin that Luke puts on the parable of the talents in Lk. 19:11–27; see also 2 Pet. 3). Jesus himself awaits the full manifestation of the kingdom, telling his disciples on the night before his death that he "will never again drink of this fruit of the vine until that day when I drink it new with you in my Father's kingdom" (Mt. 26:29). First, the "good news of the kingdom" must be spread throughout the world, the yeast through the whole lump of dough, before the end arrives (Mt. 24:14). In the interim, it falls to the disciples to carry out this task as witnesses of the kingdom (Acts 1:6–8) and to remain faithful in the midst of an age shared by the righteous and unrighteous, awaiting the day when God's angels will sort good from bad and invite the former into the fullness of God's kingdom (see Mt. 13:24–30, 36–43; 47–50). In this in-between time, believers are to remind themselves of the goal for which they long and for which they are to prepare themselves each time they pray "Your kingdom come" (Mt. 6:10).

The Cosmic Battle

A second, pervasive component of the "apocalyptic" dimension of the New Testament is its focus on the activities of angelic and demonic powers and their intersection with the lives of believers. Discipleship and community were lived out not only in the context of a larger, chronological story of God's kingdom breaking in and moving on to consummation but also in the context of a rather active cosmology. As people looked "up" or "down" from the human sphere of activity, they were invited to consider the agendas and activities of angelic and demonic forces, engaged in a cosmic struggle over the world of human beings.

The struggle began in the primeval history of the sacred story, although the origins of the struggle remain mysterious. Intertestamental Jewish texts (notably *1 Enoch* and *Jubilees*, which appear to have left their mark on 2 Pet. 2:4 and Jude 6) look to the defection from their proper place of numerous angels who sought intercourse with human women (see Gen. 6:1–4) as the beginning of the conflict. From the illicit union of these angels with human females arose the "giants," and the souls of these hybrid offspring became the demons that plague humankind. Other texts look to the rebellion of Satan against God, to his expulsion from heaven (see Lk. 10:18), and to Satan's presence in the Garden of Eden as his first assault on humankind (Gen. 3 appears to be read thus in Rev. 12:9). Whichever story an early Jew or Christian heard and accepted, he or she saw the world as caught up in the midst of a long-standing conflict between unseen, spiritual forces that could powerfully impact daily life. This backdrop provides an interpretative framework for many events experienced in the human sphere, from illness to vicious acts to church conflict, as well as a source of motivation to take certain courses of action that will advance the cause of God and hinder the plans of "the Enemy."

Jesus enters the scene as a mighty combatant in this conflict. John summarizes his ministry in these terms: "The Son of God was revealed for this purpose, to destroy the works of the devil" (1 Jn. 3:8). Throughout the gospels, Jesus and Satan are depicted as antagonists. Satan attempts to lead Jesus into sin, encountering him in the desert in single combat, as it were (Mt. 4:1–11; Lk. 4:1–13). Jesus resists each of Satan's temptations, his answers revealing his commitment and obedience to God's word. From that point on, Jesus (joined eventually by his disciples) wages a campaign against the forces of Satan, casting demons from the people they afflicted and dominated (see Mk. 1:21–28, 34; 3:11; 5:1–20; 6:13; 7:24–30; 9:14–29). Jesus speaks of this campaign thus: "No one can enter a strong man's house and plunder his property without first tying up the strong man; then indeed the house can be plundered" (Mk. 3:27). Jesus has bound his antagonist and now takes back all those whom Satan's minions sought to possess (see the summary statement in Acts 10:38).

Evangelists Luke and John understand Satan to be at work again in the arrest and execution of Jesus, particularly in Judas' betrayal of Jesus, which is directly attributed to Satan's inspiration and even possession (Lk. 22:3; John 13:2, 26–30). As the wheels of the arrest and trial are set in motion, Jesus comments that "the ruler of this world is coming" (Jn. 14:30), but Satan is deceived about the significance of the events about to take place. He has no real power over Jesus (Jn. 14:30–31), and the crucifixion will have a rather different effect: "now is the judgment of this world; now the ruler of this world will be driven out" (Jn. 12:31). Through his obedience to God to the point of death, Jesus will effect a surprising victory over the adversary: "Since, therefore, the children share flesh and blood, he himself likewise shared the same things, so that through death he might destroy the one who has the power of death, that is, the devil, and free those who all their lives were held in slavery by the fear of death" (Heb. 2:14–15).

Despite his defeat, Satan continues to play a role in the remainder of history until the judgment. In Jesus' parables, he is said to sow the tares into the field (that is, to pervert humanity and lead some away from obedience into wickedness; see Mt. 13:24–30, 36–43) and steal the saving word from the hearts of the unwary (Mt. 13:3–9, 18–23). His work as a deceiver, leading people and nations astray from the truth, and as an antagonist to God's work in bringing together a redeemed people in the church will continue to be emphasized throughout the New Testament (see 2 Cor. 4:3–4; 11:12–15; Rev. 20:3, 10). His end, however, is presented as certain: together with his angels, who are themselves being reserved for punishment (2 Pet. 2:4; Jude 6), he will ultimately be imprisoned in a place of torment created for him (Mt. 25:41; Rev. 20:10).

Jesus' struggle against Satan and his forces is repeated in the lives of the believers, who are themselves equipped with all that is needed to share in Jesus' victory over the adversary. With the battle lines clearly drawn between good and evil, between Christ and Satan, particular courses of action may be presented to believing communities as strategic and even necessary in light of the martial situation within which they live. As the disciple considers a course of action in light of the broader context of the cosmic conflict, he or she will be more likely to adopt the course recommended or eschew the course discouraged.

The larger canvas of the spiritual forces at war with one another is frequently invoked in order to regulate behavior within the group or to reinforce the boundaries of the group. The Christian is regularly reminded of the conflict around him or her and of the call to "conquer" the adversary (see Jas. 4:7–8; 1 Jn. 2:12–14; 3:8–9). In perhaps one of the more celebrated passages concerned with "spiritual warfare," the author of Ephesians calls on the Christian to fully arm himself or herself with the core values of the Christian culture for the daily conflict with Satan (see Eph. 6:10–18). The invisible war may also be used to motivate some very specific, group-building and group-defining behaviors. Ephesians, for example, motivates the disciples to dispel anger within the group speedily, rather than hold grudges, by calling their attention to the greater enemy without: "Be angry but do not sin; do not let the sun go down on your anger, and do not make room for the devil" (Eph. 4:26–27). The author's implication here is that unresolved anger within the group opens up an avenue of attack for their common spiritual enemy. The defenses of the community may be rendered vulnerable by breaches in interpersonal relations, and concern for the good of the whole group should lead to quick and amicable reconciliation. The same passage will go on to warn also against grieving the Holy Spirit in the midst of the community by harboring bitterness and malice against a fellow believer (Eph. 4:30–32). The behaviors believers pursue and attitudes they harbor are to be chosen with a view to how these will affect their stand in the cosmic struggle, neither giving quarter to the adversary nor driving away or alienating their great Ally.

Similar issues are addressed by Paul in 2 Corinthians 2:5–11. A single believer had attacked Paul's authority, apparently after having been impressed and won over by rival teachers. Responding to a letter by Paul (now lost), the congregation rebuked this believer, thus affirming their commitment to Paul. Paul now writes that they should forgive the offender and restore him to fellowship, affirming Paul's forgiveness of him. The motivation Paul adduces, however, is rooted in the cosmic conflict: "And we do this so that we may not be outwitted by Satan; for we are not ignorant of his designs" (2 Cor. 2:11). Once again, rifts in the community of believers are warned against as a point of vulnerability in the face of the greater adversary. It is the disciples' responsibility to ensure the strength of the community by practicing mutual forgiveness, as well as to reclaim the individual temporarily won over by Satan through false teachers or through wandering from the truth of the gospel (see, for example, 2 Tim. 2:24–26).

The cosmic conflict also permits the clear division of the world into opposing camps, as it were. John gives voice to this conviction in his first epistle: "We know that we are God's children, and that the whole world lies under the power of the evil one" (1 Jn. 5:19). The boundaries of the group are strongly reinforced by such a depiction of reality. The community of disciples constitutes God's family, while the whole environment in which the church finds itself is labeled the sphere of Satan's dominion. John thus leads the hearers to consider themselves in an adversarial position vis-à-vis the surrounding society, even to consider separation and difference from that society a positive good, given the infernal allegiance of the surrounding world.

The cosmic struggle between the believing community and the spiritual adversary becomes an interpretative framework for the experience of society's opposition to and censure of converts to the new faith. The congregations addressed by 1 Peter are led to view their struggle to remain firm in their commitment to Jesus in the face of society's hostility as a struggle not to yield to Satan, not to be defeated by him:

> Discipline yourselves, keep alert. Like a roaring lion your adversary the devil prowls around, looking for someone to devour. Resist him, steadfast in your faith, for you know that your brothers and sisters in all the world are undergoing the same kinds of suffering. (1 Pet. 5:8–9)

The apocalyptic dimensions of their experience make resistance to the pressures to assimilate back into the dominant culture all the more critical, because such assimilation would mean not merely rejoining their non-Christian neighbors (fellow human beings) but being defeated and destroyed–ingestion being a powerful, negative synonym for assimilation—by the archenemy of God.

The boundaries between sect and society will repeatedly be reinforced by redrawing the landscape as a war zone between the forces of God and the forces of wickedness. Perhaps no New Testament text does this as dramatically or effectively as Revelation. The Christians addressed in the seven churches in the Roman province of Asia (what is now western Turkey) faced a variety of challenges, such as pressure from the society to assimilate once more into the behaviors of the dominant culture (e.g., idolatry, emperor cult), hostility from the local synagogues, and preachers of a form of Christianity that made room for the concessions to idolatrous worship demanded of good citizens by the outside world. Some congregations were apparently so caught up in the prosperity of the Roman economy that they failed to express a different voice from their society and so were censured as "lukewarm" or "dead" (Rev. 3:1, 16). Some, however, diligently preserved their distinctive witness and suffered a variety of forms of social pressure as a result—from slander to impending imprisonment and a single violent death (Rev. 2:9–10, 13).

To Christians facing a broad spectrum of challenges, then, John issues his pastoral and prophetic word in the form of an apocalypse, a revelation from beyond this observable world of that broader context within which to interpret daily events and choices. The believers find themselves in the midst of an age-long war between "Michael and his angels" and the "dragon and his angels" (Rev. 12:7–8), with the latter having already been defeated and cast down from heaven. The defeated enemy now devotes himself to persecuting the people of God (Rev. 2:10, 13; 12:17) and leading unbelievers astray by means of the cult of the emperor and other idolatrous forms of worship, which are, in effect, worship of Satan himself (Rev. 9:20; 13:1–18). This has a stunning effect on the way in which the believers are oriented toward their world and particular realities within it. No longer do they see fellow human beings pressuring them to conform to the dominant culture or to acknowledge the debt of gratitude understood to be due the emperor, but rather they see the machine of God's enemy at work. This machine is trying to rob them of their crown in God's eternal kingdom, and they are called to achieve a victory over the cosmic enemy by remaining steadfast in their witness to the One God and in their refusal of all idolatrous cults (see, for example, Rev. 14:6–13 and 15:2–4).

The backdrop of cosmic conflict again heightens the seriousness of the choices to be made. It is not a matter of religious preferences or cultural sensitivities that is at stake, but conquering or being conquered by the evil one. Knowing the outcome of the conflict, affirmed throughout the hymns of Revelation and so dramatically portrayed in Revelation 19–20, also impels the hearers to choose against a course that, in effect, makes peace with God's adversary. In light of Satan's final defeat and punishment (together with all those who were taken in by him, Rev. 20:7–10, 14–15) and in light of the rewards to be enjoyed by those who sided with the Conqueror, deprivation and death now can be accounted a glorious victory over the enemy (even as in human wars many on the winning side will die).

The New Testament authors do not speak merely of spiritual forces of wickedness, however, in their construction of the Christian worldview. Alongside Satan and his angels one finds spiritual powers that may range from good to neutral to evil (such as the "elemental spirits of the universe" in Gal. 4:8–9 and Col. 2:8, 15; and the "authorities and powers" subjected to Christ in 1 Pet. 3:22), but also hosts of spiritual beings loyal and subservient to God's will. These are the more familiar angels, who serve as messengers, bringing God's word to human beings (see Mt. 1:20, 24; 2:13, 19; 28:2, 5; Acts 8:26). As such, they are also popularly associated with having given the Torah to Moses from God, a tradition that grew up alongside the tradition that Moses received it from God face-to-face (see Acts 7:53; Gal. 3:19; Heb. 2:1–2). They are often cast in the role of protectors and servants, helping God's people on earth (Mt. 4:11; Acts 5:19; 12:7–11; Heb. 1:14).

The angels, together with the quite varied inhabitants of God's throne room (the seven archangels, the "spirits of the presence" in Rev. 4:5; 8:2; the "four living creatures" that probably represent the cherubim in Rev. 4:6–8; the twenty-four elders, the order referred to elsewhere as "thrones," in

Rev. 4:4), also perform heavenly liturgies. It is Revelation that brings this aspect of their activity most forcefully to the fore (see Rev. 4:1–5:14; 7:11–12; 11:15–18; 19:1–8), reminding the worshipers on earth—the obvious minority in the midst of the unbelieving society—that they are properly attuned to the worship of the hosts of heaven, that they gather in harmony with the cosmic majority as they continue steadfast in their assemblies together.

Finally, angels are also depicted as a powerful army, arrayed and organized for battle (Mt. 26:53; Rev. 12:7–8). They are a formidable force whose victory over Satan and his legions has already been realized, and who now stand ready to assist God in the final judgment. To them the New Testament authors assign the tasks of administering God's end-time plagues and judgments on the world (see Rev. 7:1–2; 8:1–6; 15:1–8; 16:1–12, 17), separating the wicked from the righteous (Mt. 13:24–30, 36–43), executing judgment on the sinners (Rev. 14:14–20), and conducting the righteous to their reward (Mt. 24:31). Once again, the Christian group is reminded by such texts that they are not, in fact, a powerless, deviant minority, but rather that the indefatigable forces of heaven stand ready for God's signal to vindicate them before the whole world.

The Hour of God's Judgment

A focal point of early Christian expectation was the day of judgment, a point of continuity with the Old Testament expectation of the "day of the Lord," God's breaking into human history in all God's holiness and justice to set matters right. The New Testament's focus on this forthcoming day connects with the universalism theme of the Old Testament, as the God of the Christian community and of historic Israel shows God's Self to be God of history and God of the world. In the words of Revelation, "The kingdom of the world has become the kingdom of our Lord and of his Messiah," and that Lord executes justice upon the whole world (Rev. 11:15).

The fact of God's judgment and triumphant reign (whether expressed as the day of judgment or as the consummation of the journey begun at conversion) is everywhere affirmed in the New Testament as a reliable coordinate with regard to which the believer is to shape his or her life and train his or her ambitions. This is remembered by the evangelists as part of the proclamation of Jesus (see Mt. 7:21–23; 11:20–24; 12:36, 41–42; 13:24–30, 36–43, 47–50; etc.), of his forerunner John the Baptist (Mt. 3:7–12), and of his apostles (Acts 17:30–31). The judgment of God also features prominently in the teaching of Paul and his team (Rom. 2:3–11; 1 Cor. 4:5; 2 Cor. 5:9–10; Phil. 1:6, 10–11; 3:10–11, 14, 21; 1 Thess. 1:9–10; 3:13; 4:13–18; 5:23–24; 1 Tim. 6:14–15; 2 Tim. 4:7–8) and in the teaching of John the Seer (see Rev. 1:7; 11:15–18; 14:7, 14–20; 20:11–15; 22:12). It appears to have been a standard element of the catechesis (the instruction of new converts) in the early church (Heb. 6:1–2; *Didache* 16). After the death of the first generation of believers, it appears that the certainty of God's visitation to judge the world was called into question. The author of 2 Peter addresses such a scenario:

> First of all you must understand this, that in the last days scoffers will come, scoffing and indulging their own lusts and saying, "Where is the promise of his coming? For ever since our ancestors died, all things continue as they were from the beginning of creation!" They deliberately ignore this fact, that by the word of God heavens existed long ago and an earth was formed out of water and by means of water, through which the world of that time was deluged with water and perished. But by the same word the present heavens and earth have been reserved for fire, being kept until the day of judgment and destruction of the godless. (2 Pet. 3:3–7)

The flood story becomes a resource for this early church leader to demonstrate the reliability of the oracles of Jesus and of the Old Testament prophets that speak of a day of judgment. Just as God was able and determined to interrupt the course of human history because of human sinfulness in the days of Noah, so God has purposed to do so again when it shall please God. Doubting God's justice (and intent to bring justice to the earth) is itself seen as a sign of the "last days." It is only God's patience (see also Rom. 2:4) that delays God's enactment of God's essential character as a just God.

All are already accountable to the One God, whether or not they acknowledge God. God's act of beneficence in creating the heavens and earth and all people, as well as richly providing the people food and habitations, indebted all humanity to show God the thanks and honor that were God's due (Acts 17:30–31; Rev. 14:6–7). In this regard, a Christian would agree with the dominant culture's emphasis on piety as a cardinal virtue, although doing so agrees with the Jewish critique of that culture, namely, giving the thanks and reverence due the One God to lifeless idols and created things (Rom. 1:18–32; Rev. 9:20; 16:9). Their refusal to obey this God and throw away their idols, as well as their refusal to live in obedience to this God's commands, renders them liable to God's judgment (1 Pet. 4:4–6). Failure to recognize the claims of this God does not free them from being judged and punished by God for their impieties. God's universal reign will be manifest in the punishment of God's opponents as well as in the reward of God's faithful, reverent children.

It was only as the believers looked ahead to the future acts of God that they found a resolution for the tension between the believers' sense of their identity (e.g., God's faithful servants) and their experience (e.g., dishonored and marginalized by their society). On the day of judgment, at Christ's return, their own honor and the virtue of their commitments and choices would be revealed to all who presently censured and abused them, while the error of those who refused to turn to God with obedient hearts would be manifest as well (2 Thess. 1:5–12). The hope for vindication was not based merely on a desire for being proven right; it was grounded in the early church's understanding of God's character as a just God who would punish wickedness and reward virtue. When people are killed precisely because they act out of regard for God's honor and standards, a just God cannot refuse indefinitely to act.

Perhaps Revelation affords us the most vivid picture of this aspect of the New Testament's message:

> I saw under the altar the souls of those who had been slaughtered for the word of God and for the testimony they had given; they cried out with a loud voice, "Sovereign Lord, holy and true, how long will it be before

> you judge and avenge our blood on the inhabitants of the earth?" They were each given a white robe and told to rest a little longer, until the number would be complete both of their fellow servants and of their brothers and sisters, who were soon to be killed as they themselves had been killed. (Rev. 6:9–11)

The God who is celebrated here as holy and true cannot, in the end, prove untrue to God's faithful clients who have suffered dishonor, injustice, and even death for God's cause. Later in Revelation, using language borrowed heavily from the Old Testament, God will be praised as "just":

> They sing the song of Moses, the servant of God, and the song of the Lamb: "Great and amazing are your deeds, Lord God the Almighty! Just and true are your ways, King of the nations! Lord, who will not fear and glorify your name? For you alone are holy. All nations will come and worship before you, for your judgments have been revealed." (Rev. 15:3–4)

As John narrates a future in which God's judgments for God's people against the enemies of God are played out, he expresses his hope and conviction that the old songs about God–God's power, justice, and truth manifesting themselves in God's judicial actions on behalf of God's people and against God's adversaries–will be renewed in the future. John's narration of the future celebrations of those who will emerge victorious from the present contest carries with it the implicit claim that the unfolding future will demonstrate the ongoing validity and reliability of the convictions about God articulated in those ancient songs. God's justice and power will consistently result in God's actions against the unjust and on behalf of those who do justice (i.e., "keep the commandments of God and hold fast to the faith of Jesus," Rev. 14:12).

The proclamation of God's forthcoming judgment in Revelation was also a direct, frontal assault on the dominant culture. Looking ahead to that day when God will set things right does not mean turning a blind eye to what is wrong in the here and now; on the contrary, it provides an avenue by which to offer prophetic critique of a society that tramples on God's desire for all people. In Revelation 17–18, John holds up the Roman system to the light of God's vision for humanity. In the face of the Roman imperial ideology, which proclaims Roman rule to be the beneficent vehicle by which the gods' favor comes to the inhabited world, the agent of order, peace, and prosperity, John denounces Rome as a new Babylon. Its peace and order are plastered with the mortar of blood; its prosperity is one in which the few enjoy the depths of conspicuous consumption while the many live at subsistence level. The economic injustice of the new order, the self-glorification of Rome as the hope of the world (expressed most visibly in the worship of the goddess *Roma* alongside the emperors throughout Asia Minor), and especially the violence on which Roman rule is founded are what John holds up as crying out for God's judgment and punitive action (Rev. 17:6; 18:2–8, 23–24; 19:2):

> I heard the angel of the waters say, "You are just, O Holy One, who are and were, for you have judged these things; because they shed the blood of saints and prophets, you have given them blood to drink. It is what they deserve!" And I heard the altar respond, "Yes, O Lord God, the Almighty, your judgments are true and just!" (16:5–7)

Those victims of human injustice encountered in Revelation 6:9–11 will thus, at the end, acclaim God's justice.

The certainty of God's intervention to judge the world and to recreate the world is established not only by God's justice but also by God's faithfulness to God's purposes for the world and for God's faithful ones. Paul celebrates in two places the full scope of God's promise for God's people and God's whole creation. In 1 Corinthians 15:20–28, Paul looks ahead beyond the resurrection of the dead to the final triumph of Christ over every power and enemy, climaxing in the defeat of death itself, which was not part of God's original purpose for creation. The future intervention of God means that, in the words of John Donne, "Death, thou shalt die" (from Donne's poem, "Death Be Not Proud"). In Romans 8:18–23, Paul speaks of the whole creation's "groaning in labor pains until now," waiting "with eager longing for the revealing of the children of God." Not only will the children of God benefit from God's future acts, but "creation itself will be set free from its bondage to decay and will obtain the freedom of the glory of the children of God." God's triumph will be manifest in the renewal and transformation of the whole creation to which God committed God's Self when God created the heavens and the earth—not to abandon it to the forces of sin and death, but to redeem all that belongs to God.

The author of Hebrews and the author of Revelation devote considerable space to describing the place prepared for, and final state of, the faithful children of God (see Heb. 6:19–20; 4:1–11; 11:11–16; 13:14; Rev. 21:1–22:5; 7:14–17). Both these authors derive their respective pictures of that future state from their conviction that God is faithful to God's promises, made to God's people of old. For example, John remembers, and reminds his hearers of, God's promise that "my dwelling place shall be with them; and I will be their God, and they shall be my people... My sanctuary is among them forever" (Ezek. 37:27–28; cf. Rev. 21:3) and that "GOD will wipe away the tears from all faces" as God causes "sorrow and sighing" to "flee away" (Isa. 25:8; 35:10; cf. Rev. 21:4). The existence of such promises combined with the conviction that God stands by God's promises unfailingly leads, in effect, to the future that John posits, a future in which God's purposes and vision for God's people become a reality.

Living at the Threshold of Two Ages

Throughout the New Testament, this imminent (at least, sufficiently imminent) visitation of God and God's Anointed One for judgment is presented as a crisis for which the hearers, who have been given insider knowledge that this crisis is coming, must prepare diligently in the present. Deliberations within the early church are consistently oriented toward preparing for that day, allowing for the new agenda of discipleship and commitment to one another in the Christian community to replace any competing agendas imposed by society or by the individual's desires to "get along" in society. It is important to these authors that the "day of the Lord" neither be collapsed into the present day (2 Thess. 2:1–2) nor be seen as a distant or doubtful event (2 Pet. 3:3–7). Rather, it is upheld throughout as the one certain future event in light of which each day must be lived, no matter how many days that may be. Even if "imminence" comes to be doubted, the "suddenness" of the coming of that day remains intact throughout the New Testament. The lack of warning, whenever the day of judgment does finally arrive (see Mt. 24:36–44; 1 Thess. 5:3–4), calls for preparedness for this crisis to be at the center of each day "as long as it is called 'today'" (Heb. 3:12–14).

Preparation for that day involves, first and foremost, putting away from oneself all those behaviors and attitudes that have invited God's wrath, the wrath that will be poured out in judgment against the disobedient (see Acts 3:19–21; Col. 3:5–11, note especially Col. 3:6). In the sight of God, the impartial judge, the imperative is simply to do what is good and avoid all manner of disobedience and vice (Rom. 2:1–11). Since the day is already beginning to dawn, there is no room for making provisions for the passions of the flesh, whether carnal desires or relational sins, such as quarreling, envy, and grumbling (Rom. 13:11–14; Jas. 5:9). Instead, the early church leaders urge the disciples to strive for holiness and blamelessness before God, using each day the end is delayed as a gift from God to repent and press forward toward holiness (2 Pet. 3:8–15a, 17–18). The interim period is a time for the disciples to use the resources entrusted to them as God's stewards for the bearing of fruit for God's kingdom, and for preparing to meet the King by doing good now to "the least of these my brothers and sisters" (Mt. 25:14–46). The author of 1 Peter invokes the coming crisis as a mandate for maintaining self-discipline, mutual love (which "covers a multitude of sins"—something valuable on the day of judgment), and hospitality; using whatever gifts one has received for the good of the community of disciples; helping one another hold on till that day; and keeping focused on readiness for that day (1 Pet. 4:7–11). It is urgent to keep reminding fellow believers to make their life choices in light of the coming day, as well as to keep calling unbelievers to repent and prepare (2 Tim. 4:1–2).

The day of judgment provides early church leaders with a tremendous resource for helping their congregations resist the pressures put on them by their non-Christian neighbors to resume the way of life that they have left behind. The author of Hebrews, for example, repeatedly underscores the imperative to remain steadfast in loyalty and witness to Jesus, rather than shrink back in the face of society's opposition (Heb. 10:37–39). A far greater crisis looms on the horizon than lost property or censure and abuse from human beings—namely, the encounter of all people with the Living God as Judge and Avenger (Heb. 10:26–31; 12:25–29). It would be distinctly disadvantageous on that day to have made peace now with those who oppose God. There is also the encouragement, however, that comes from contemplating the good things—the abiding homeland, city, and honor—that God has prepared for the loyal sons and daughters (Heb. 2:10; 4:1–11; 10:19–22, 34–36; 11:10, 13–16; 12:28; 13:14). Knowing that God will vindicate God's loyal sons and daughters on that day enables endurance in the face of hardship, and even a willingness to embrace society's hostility toward the faithful as a means by which their loyalty and character are sharpened and shown to be tried and true, resulting in "praise and honor and renown" on that day (1 Pet. 1:6–7; see also 2 Thess. 1:4–5; Jas. 5:7–11.

The radical break between "this present, evil age" that is "passing away" and the coming age of God's eternal, abiding kingdom calls for a corresponding break with one's attachment to the pursuits, values, and goods of this visible (and temporary) world in favor of seeking that which abides, attaching oneself to those commitments, behaviors, internal attitudes, and external relationships that link one with the coming age. This is apparent in texts that speak of the disciples as having "stripped off the old self with its practices" and having clothed themselves "with the new self" (Col. 3:9–10; see also Eph. 4:22–24) or with Christ (see Rom. 13:11–14), or as having died to one way of life and being raised or reborn to a new way of life (Rom. 6:1–14).

Paul emphasizes quite forcefully the detachment that the disciples are to have from the things of this age in 1 Corinthians 7:29–31:

> The appointed time has grown short; from now on, let even those who have wives be as though they had none, and those who mourn as though they were not mourning, and those who rejoice as though they were not rejoicing,

> and those who buy as though they had no possessions, and those who deal with the world as though they had no dealings with it. For the present form of this world is passing away.

The transient nature of this present age must be kept in view in all the disciples' dealings with the world—its business, its joys, its sorrows, even its legitimate institutions such as marriage—so that these things do not distract the believers from the "true" reality that is about to manifest itself as this age finally dissolves and God's kingdom comes into being. In this chapter, Paul legitimately recognizes that one of the greatest hindrances to discipleship is not gross sin, but allowing the present world to be "too much with us." Those who are overly devoted to the business and affairs of this world, however, belie the very truth that stands at the heart of Jesus' gospel: The kingdom of God is at hand.

The transient nature of the present world and the eternal nature of the age to come establish the relative value of this world and the next, such that Paul willingly accepts the deprivations and hardships encountered here as a result of seeking to arrive there (2 Cor. 4:16–5:10). For no joy of earth would he sacrifice the joy of the coming age, and he invites his congregations to adopt that mind-set. The author of Colossians also calls for (and enables) separation from the goals and desires connected to this world by calling attention to the believers' placement with Jesus already in the age to come, freeing the disciple for single-hearted pursuit of the agenda of discipleship: "Set your minds on things that are above, not on things that are on earth, for you have died, and your life is hidden with Christ in God. When Christ who is your life is revealed, then you also will be revealed with him in glory" (Col. 3:2–4).

The knowledge of what is to come separates the believer not only from the way of life that characterized his or her past but also from those who have refused the message and even try to pressure the Christians to live once more "as if" God were not coming to judge the world. As Paul depicts this state of affairs, however, it is not the harassed Christians but the harassing unbelievers who are, in reality, the disfavored and disprivileged ones:

> The day of the Lord will come like a thief in the night. When they say, "There is peace and security," then sudden destruction will come upon them, as labor pains come upon a pregnant woman, and there will be no escape! But you, beloved, are not in darkness, for that day to surprise you like a thief; for you are all children of light and children of the day; we are not of the night or of darkness. So then let us not fall asleep as others do, but let us keep awake and be sober; for those who sleep sleep at night, and those who are drunk get drunk at night. But since we belong to the day, let us be sober...For God has destined us not for wrath but for obtaining salvation through our Lord Jesus Christ. (1 Thess. 5:2–9)

Christians may look on the way of life that they left behind, and the way of life that their neighbors pressure them to resume, as the equivalent of walking about in a drunken stupor or groping about in the dark. Having been granted knowledge of the impending crisis, and having turned to God and God's Messiah in repentance and obedience, the disciples have awakened from that stupor and "seen the light" about the reality of their world. Such images assist them not only to persevere in preparation for the day but also to resist the daily pressures on them to return to their pre-Christian way of life. The vision of the triumph of God thus powerfully enables both discipleship and the survival of the community.

The New Testament authors thus set their congregations between the cross on which Jesus died on their behalf and the clouds on which Jesus will return to gather them into God's kingdom. In the words of the author of the Letter to Titus,

> For the grace of God has appeared, bringing salvation to all, training us to renounce impiety and worldly passions, and in the present age to live lives that are self-controlled, upright, and godly, while we wait for the blessed hope and the manifestation of the glory of our great God and Savior, Jesus Christ. He it is who gave himself for us that he might redeem us from all iniquity and purify for himself a people of his own who are zealous for good deeds. (Titus 2:11–14)

The new initiative of God's kindness revealed in the death and resurrection of Jesus begins the process by which Christians are prepared for the benefits God has decreed for God's people. In their cleansing from past sins and their being set apart for God, the believers begin their journey of discipleship, pressing forward in solidarity with one another to that consummation of God's grace, the final deliverance ("salvation," Heb. 1:14; 9:28; 1 Pet. 1:5) on the day of God's triumph. The passage from Titus above beautifully holds together the two main coordinates of the Christian life, set as the compass points for each day: living in a way that honors the gift Jesus gave in his death and that preserves one for his coming again.

As the readers of the New Testament texts kept their eyes firmly on these fixed points and charted their courses accordingly, they discovered "stability" (2 Pet. 3:17) in the midst of the waves of doubt, of their own passions, and of hostility from those who did not share their vision. Journeying forward to "enter God's rest," the divine realm where Christ has already entered as their forerunner, remains at the fore of the believers' agenda, bringing a single-mindedness and integrity to all life experience. The disciples are called ever to continue their movement out from being at home in the world toward Jesus, bearing censure and abuse for the sake of him who bore a cross for them, because that is the movement that leads to the abiding city and eternal safety when God comes to judge (Heb. 4:1–11; 13:12–14).

For Further Reading

Introductions to the New Testament

Barr, David. *The New Testament Story: An Introduction.* 2d ed. Belmont, Calif.: Wadsworth, 1995.

Drane, John. *Introducing the New Testament.* San Francisco: Harper and Row, 1986.

Johnson, Luke T. *The Writings of the New Testament: An Interpretation.* 2d ed., rev. Minneapolis: Fortress Press, 1999.

Patzia, Arthur G. *The Making of the New Testament: Origin, Collection, Text and Canon.* Downers Grove, Ill.: InterVarsity Press, 1995.

Pregeant, Russell. *Engaging the New Testament: An Interdisciplinary Approach.* Minneapolis: Fortress Press, 1995.

The World of the New Testament

Bell, Albert A. *Exploring the New Testament World.* Nashville: Thomas Nelson, 1998.

deSilva, David A. *Honor, Patronage, Purity, Kinship: Unlocking New Testament Culture.* Downers Grove, Ill.: InterVarsity Press, 2000.

———. *The Hope of Glory: Honor Discourse and New Testament Interpretation.* Collegeville, Minn.: Liturgical Press, 1999.

Ferguson, Everett C. *Backgrounds of Early Christianity.* 2d ed., rev. Grand Rapids, Mich.: Eerdmans, 1993.

Malina, Bruce A. *The New Testament World.* 2d ed., rev. Louisville, Ky.: Westminster/John Knox Press, 1993.

Neyrey, Jerome H., ed. *The Social World of Luke-Acts: Models for Interpretation.* Peabody, Mass.: Hendrickson, 1991.

Stambaugh, J. E., and D. L. Balch. *The New Testament in Its Social Environment.* LEC 2. Philadelphia: Westminster Press, 1986.

Grace: The Favor of God

Danker, Frederick W. *Benefactor: Epigraphic Study of a Graeco-Roman and New Testament Semantic Field.* St. Louis: Clayton Publishing House, 1982.

deSilva, David A. *Honor, Patronage, Kinship, and Purity: Unlocking New Testament Culture.* Downers Grove, Ill.: InterVarsity Press, 2000.

Moxnes, H. "Patron-Client Relations and the New Community in Luke-Acts." In *The Social World of Luke-Acts,* edited by J. H. Neyrey, 241–68. Peabody, Mass.: Hendrickson, 1991.

Seneca. *On Benefits (De beneficiis).* In *Seneca: Moral Essays,* translated by J. W. Basore. Vol. 3. Cambridge: Harvard University Press, 1958.

Discipleship: The Way of God

Bonhoeffer, Dietrich. *The Cost of Discipleship.* New York: Macmillan, 1963.

Longenecker, Richard N., ed. *Patterns of Discipleship in the New Testament.* Grand Rapids, Mich.: Eerdmans, 1996.

Schweizer, Eduard. *Lordship and Discipleship.* Studies in Biblical Theology 28. Naperville, Ill.: Alec R. Allenson, 1960.

Segovia, Fernando, ed. *Discipleship in the New Testament.* Philadelphia: Fortress Press, 1985.

Wilkins, M. J. *Following the Master: Discipleship in the Steps of Jesus.* Grand Rapids, Mich.: Zondervan, 1991.

Church: The People of God

Banks, Robert. *Paul's Idea of Community: The Early House Churches in their Historical Setting.* Grand Rapids, Mich.: Eerdmans, 1980.

deSilva, David A. *Honor, Patronage, Kinship, and Purity: Unlocking New Testament Culture.* Downers Grove, Ill.: InterVarsity Press, 2000.

Giles, K. N. *What on Earth is the Church? A Biblical and Theological Inquiry.* Downers Grove, Ill.: InterVarsity Press, 1995.

Kee, Howard C. *Who Are the People of God? Early Christian Models of Community.* New Haven, Conn.: Yale University Press, 1995.

Apocalypticism: The Triumph of God

Allison, Dale C. *The End of the Ages Has Come.* Philadelphia: Fortress Press, 1987.

Beker, J. Christiaan. *The Triumph of God: The Essence of Paul's Thought.* Minneapolis, Minn.: Fortress Press, 1990.

Carey, Greg, and L. Gregory Bloomquist, eds. *Vision and Persuasion: Rhetorical Dimensions of Apocalyptic Discourse.* St. Louis: Chalice Press, 1999.

Collins, Adela Yarbro. *Crisis and Catharsis: The Power of the Apocalypse.* Philadelphia: Westminster Press, 1984.

Collins, John J. *The Apocalyptic Imagination.* 2d ed. Grand Rapids, Mich.: Eerdmans, 1998.

Russell, D. S. *Divine Disclosure: An Introduction to Jewish Apocalyptic.* London: SCM Press, 1992.

——. *Prophecy and the Apocalyptic Dream: Protest and Promise.* Peabody, Mass.: Hendrickson, 1994.

Talbert, Charles H. *The Apocalypse: A Reading of the Revelation of John.* Louisville, Ky.: Westminster/John Knox Press, 1994.

Willis, Wendell, ed. *The Kingdom of God in 20th-century Interpretation.* Peabody, Mass.: Hendrickson, 1987.

Subject Index

Scripture and Other Ancient Literature Index

Other Ancient Literature

CPSIA information can be obtained at www.ICGtesting.com
Printed in the USA
LVOW07s1019061114

412333LV00001B/23/P